ETHIOPIA

Marxist Regimes Series

Series editor: Bogdan Szajowski,
Department of Sociology, University College, Cardiff

1 *Ethiopia* Peter Schwab

Further Titles

Afghanistan
Albania
Angola
Benin and The Congo
Bulgaria
Cape Verde, Guinea-Bissau and São Tomé and Príncipe
China
Cuba
Czechoslovakia
German Democratic Republic
Ghana
Grenada
The Co-operative Republic of Guyana
Hungary
Kampuchea
Democratic People's Republic of Korea
Laos
Madagascar
Mongolia
Mozambique
Nicaragua
Poland
Romania
Somalia
Soviet Union
Surinam
Vietnam
People's Democratic Republic of Yemen
Yugoslavia
Zimbabwe
Marxist State Governments in India
Marxist Local Governments in Western Europe and Japan
The Diversification of Communism
Comparative Analysis
Cumulative Index

ETHIOPIA

Politics, Economics and Society

Peter Schwab

Lynne Rienner Publishers, Inc.
Boulder, Colorado

First published in the United States of America in 1985 by
Lynne Rienner Publishers, Inc.,
948 North Street,
Boulder, Colorado 80302

Library of Congress Card Catalog No.84-62184
CIP Data applied for

ISBN Hardback: 0-931477-00-X
ISBN Paperback: 0-931477-01-8

Printed and bound in Great Britain by
SRP Ltd., Exeter

Editor's Preface

The study of Marxist regimes has for many years been equated with the study of communist political systems. There were several historical and methodological reasons for this.

For many years it was not difficult to distinguish the eight regimes in Eastern Europe and four in Asia which resoundingly claimed adherence to the tenets of Marxism and more particularly to their Soviet interpretation—Marxism-Leninism. These regimes, variously called 'People's Republic', 'People's Democratic Republic', or 'Democratic Republic', claimed to have derived their inspiration from the Soviet Union to which, indeed, in the overwhelming number of cases they owed their establishment.

To many scholars and analysts these regimes represented a multiplication of and geographical extension of the 'Soviet model' and consequently of the Soviet sphere of influence. Although there were clearly substantial similarities between the Soviet Union and the people's democracies, especially in the initial phases of their development, these were often overstressed at the expense of noticing the differences between these political systems.

It took a few years for scholars to realize that generalizing the particular, i.e. applying the Soviet experience to other states ruled by elites which claimed to be guided by 'scientific socialism', was not good enough. The relative simplicity of the assumption of a cohesive communist bloc was questioned after the expulsion of Yugoslavia from the Communist Information Bureau in 1948 and in particular after the workers' riots in Poznań in 1956 and the Hungarian revolution of the same year. By the mid-1960s, the totalitarian model of communist politics, which until then had been very much in force, began to crumble. As some of these regimes articulated demands for a distinctive path of socialist development, many specialists studying these systems began to notice that the cohesiveness of the communist bloc was less apparent than had been claimed before.

Also by the mid-1960s, in the newly independent African states 'democratic' multi-party states were turning into one-party states or military dictatorships, thus questioning the inherent superiority of liberal democracy, capitalism and the values that went with it. Scholars now began to ponder on the simple contrast between multi-party democracy and a one-party totalitarian rule that had satisfied an earlier generation.

More importantly, however, by the beginning of that decade Cuba had a revolution without Soviet help, a revolution which subsequently became to many political elites in the Third World not only an inspiration but a clear military, political and ideological example to follow. Apart from its romantic appeal, to many nationalist movements the Cuban revolution also demonstrated a novel way of conducting and winning a nationalist, anti-imperialist war and accepting Marxism as the state ideology without a vanguard communist party. The Cuban precedent was subsequently followed in one respect or another by scores of regimes in the Third World who used the adoption of 'scientific socialism' tied to the tradition of Marxist thought as a form of mobilization, legitimation or association with the prestigious symbols and powerful high-status regimes such as the Soviet Union, China, Cuba and Vietnam.

Despite all these changes the study of Marxist regimes remains in its infancy and continues to be hampered by constant and not always pertinent comparison with the Soviet Union, thus somewhat blurring the important underlying common theme—the 'scientific theory' of the laws of development of human society and human history. This doctrine is claimed by the leadership of these regimes to consist of the discovery of objective causal relationships; it is used to analyse the contradictions which arise between goals and actuality in the pursuit of a common destiny. Thus the political elites of these countries have been and continue to be influenced in both their ideology and their political practice by Marxism more than any other current of social thought and political practice.

The growth in the number and global significance, as well as the ideological political and economic impact, of Marxist regimes has presented scholars and students with an increasing challenge. In meeting this challenge, social scientists on both sides of the political divide have put forward a dazzling profusion of terms, models, programmes and varieties of interpretation. It is against the background of this profusion that the present comprehensive series on Marxist regimes is offered.

This collection of monographs is envisaged as a series of multidisciplinary textbooks on the governments, politics, economics and society of these countries. Each of the monographs was prepared by a specialist on the country concerned. Thus, over fifty scholars from all over the world have contributed monographs which are based on first-hand knowledge. The geographical diversity of the authors, combined with the fact that as a group they represent many disciplines of social science, gives their individual analyses and the series as a whole an additional dimension.

Each of the scholars who contributed to this series was asked to analyse such topics as the political culture, the governmental structure, the ruling party, other mass organizations, party-state relations, the policy process, the economy, domestic and foreign relations together with any features peculiar to the country under discussion.

This series does not aim at assigning authenticity or authority to any single one of the political systems included in it. It shows that depending on a variety of historical, cultural, ethnic and political factors, the pursuit of goals derived from the tenets of Marxism has produced different political forms at different times and in different places. It also illustrates the rich diversity among these societies, where attempts to achieve a synthesis between goals derived from Marxism on the one hand, and national realities, on the other, have often meant distinctive approaches and solutions to the problems of social, political and economic development.

University College
Cardiff

Bogdan Szajkowski

This book is for Ethiopia

Contents

List of Maps

List of Figures

List of Tables

Preface

This study is an analysis of the motives, policies and ideology of Ethiopia under the rule of Dergue/COPWE. It is also an attempt to impart some of the flavour of what it was like to have been witness to the first decade of revolutionary Ethiopia. What took place in 1974, when Haile Selassie I was deposed, was necessary and extraordinary; what has happened since has been both tumultuous and, for once-feudal Ethiopia, almost unbelievable. To move from feudalism to state socialism, without going through the intervening stages adopted by other recently established Marxist regimes, demands an extraordinary upheaval; and this is precisely what has taken place in Ethiopia. Although the socialist revolution was deadly for some, it has created a much freer environment for many. The peasants, former tenant-farmers, and urban proletariat are now participants in a political system that works for and represents them to a much greater degree; prior to 1974 they were merely oppressed subjects, who were at the mercy of a multitude of forces over which they had absolutely no influence. For most Ethiopians the revolution has been beneficial, as it championed their needs. A minority of the people have opposed the direction of the revolution and as a result have suffered greatly. This analysis, though a political, sociological and economic study, reflects on these recent events through a historical and ideological perspective. It should be noted too that this author is sympathetic to the direction, ideology, tone and style of the revolution. Basically, then, this book will look at what has been done, and why, and what the future direction of the revolution may be.

Although each section of the book is quite specific, there is overlap. For instance, although Chapter 2 deals with the political system, political structures are also analysed in Chapter 1. Since this is not only a structural analysis of the revolution, institutions are also discussed within ideological and historical parameters and therefore cannot be seen merely in isolation.

I would like to extend my appreciation to a number of persons who have helped make this study possible. Bogdan Szajkowski of University

College, Cardiff is certainly first on this list. As editor of this volume he asked that I take on this task and I am grateful to him. Adamantia Pollis, long ago, started me on the road of Ethiopian studies. Currently at the Graduate Faculty of the New School for Social Research, she has, as scholar and friend, emblazoned herself in my mind as the person who started me on my career. John Markakis, of the University of Crete, was one of the first Ethiopian scholars to take me under his wing and give me guidance. His friendship and writing since that time have been more than helpful. Norman Singer, an Ethiopianist now at the University of Alabama, in the past provided me with direction, and with his family, friendship and help in Ethiopia. Abdulla Adem, Eshetu Habtegiorgis, Frehot Selassie, Carol Scott, Teklemariam Kidanemariam, Frederick Clairmonte, Gwendolen Carter, Christopher Clapham, Richard Caulk, Aklilu Habte, Seamus O'Cleireacain, Susan Heck, and Ilala Ibsa have all been helpful through the years, in one way or another. Finally, I would like to extend an appreciative word to Fred Halliday and Maxine Molyneux for their remarkable book on Ethiopia, *The Ethiopian Revolution.* The last word is reserved for Stanley Millet, formerly of Adelphi University and now living in Amaguzac, Morelos, Mexico. He was always there and always supportive. He was a great friend and colleague. I miss the years that he, Marvin Surkin and I shared at Adelphi.

In 1972 I published my first book, *Decision-Making in Ethiopia*, a comprehensive account of the political process under Haile Selassie I. It is fitting that my final major work on Ethiopia should be on the new political order ushered in in 1974. Although I am a supporter of the revolution, this book is not without its criticism. In conclusion I can only say that I have always felt that it was important to be an Ethiopianist—to influence, analyse and criticize. That is what this book does.

20 April 1984
New York City

Peter Schwab

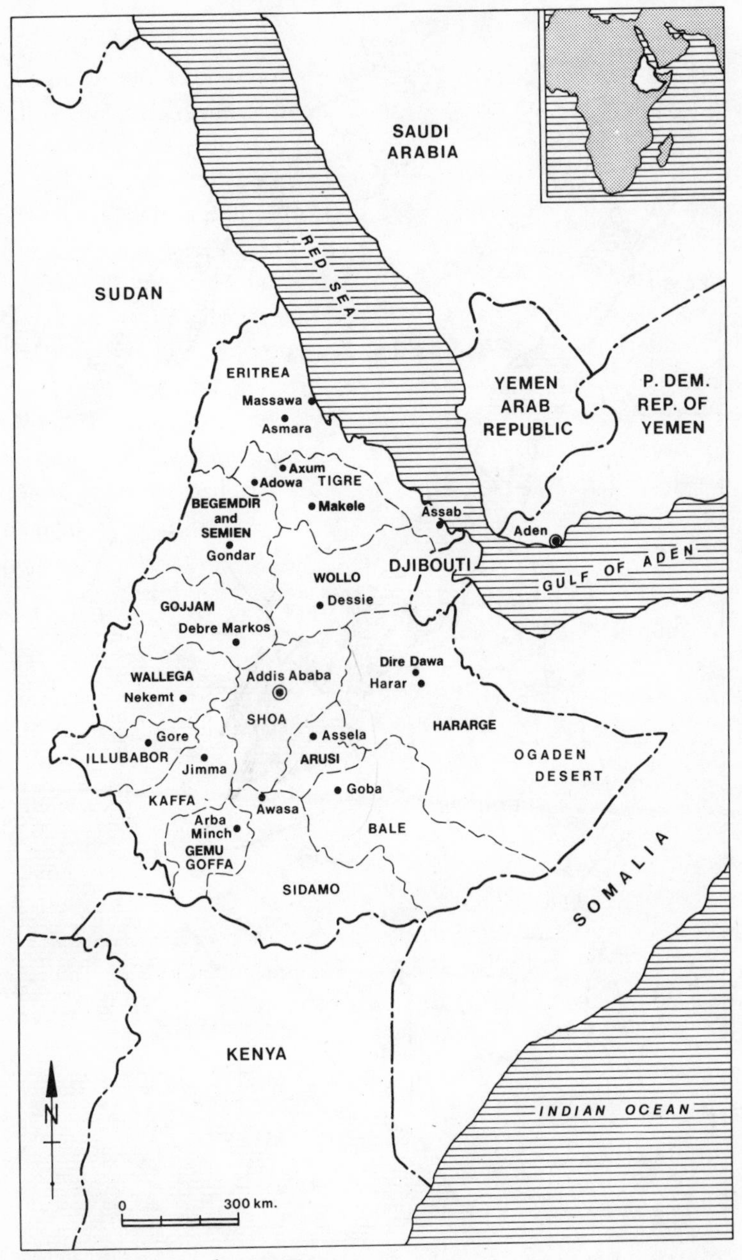

Ethiopia—Regions and Major Towns

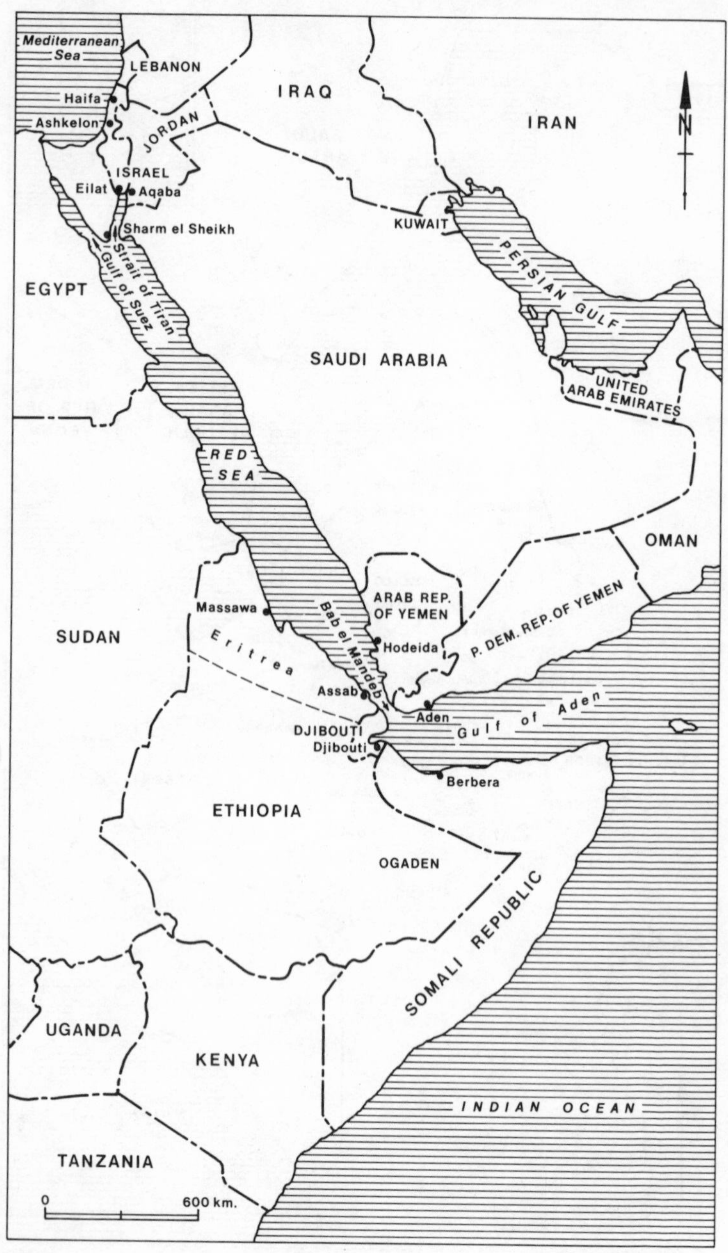

The Horn of Africa in its Geopolitical Setting

Basic Data

Official name	Ethiopia
Population	33.7 million (1984)
Population density	25 per sq. km.
Population growth (% p.a.)	2.7 (1983)
Urban population (%)	14 (1981)
Total labour force	17.5 million (1983)
Life expectancy	46 (1981)
Infant death rate (per 1,000)	145 (1981)
Child death rate (per 1,000)	31 (1981)
Ethnic groups	Amhara 19%, Oromo 40%, Tigrai 16%, Somali 6%, Sidama 6%, Shankella 4%, Gurage 2%, Afar 1%, Saho 0.5%, Agau 0.5%, Falasha 0.2%, others 4.8%
Capital	Addis Ababa—1.1 million (1983)
Land area	1,222,480 sq. km. of which 54% meadows and pastures, 8% crop-land, 7% forests, 31% desert, wasteland, water and built-on areas (1983)
Official language	Amharic
Other main languages	Tigrinya, Gallinya, Arabic
Administrative division	14 regions
Membership of international organizations	UN since 1945, OAU since 1963, CMEA observer since 1978
Foreign relations	Diplomatic and consular relations with 103 states. Representatives of 68 countries residing in Addis Ababa (1983)
Political structure	
Constitution	None
Highest legislative body	None
Highest executive body	Dergue (Provisional Military Administrative Committee) [Politburo, since September 1984]
Prime minister	None
President (Chairman of Dergue and Head of State)	Mengistu Haile Mariam (since 1977)

Ruling party	Commission to Organize the Party of the Working People of Ethiopia (COPWE). This was a pre-party organization, which in 1984 gave place to the Workers' Party.	
Secretary General of COPWE/WP	Mengistu Haile Mariam was Secretary-General of COPWE from 1979-84; then of WP.	
Party membership	Uncertain, though probably 15-30,000. Some 1,742 COPWE representatives usually attend plenary sessions.	
Growth indicators (% p.a.)	(1966-70)	(1970-81)
National income	4.4	2.2
Industry	7.4	1.8
Heavy	8.0 (est.)	2.8 (est.)
Consumer	7.8 (est.)	4.2 (est.)
Agriculture	2.2	0.9
Food production per capita	1.8 (est.)	0.4 (est.)
Trade and Balance of Payments		
Exports	US$ 374 million (1981)	
Imports	US$ 738 million (1981)	
Exports as % of GNP	8.7	
Main exports	Coffee, hides, skins, pulses and oilseeds	
Main imports (%)	Petroleum 25, machinery and transport equipment 28, food 8, other manufactures 36, other commodities 3	
Destination of exports (%)	Socialist countries 11, non-socialist countries 89 (1981)	
Main trading partners	USSR, Eastern European countries, Saudi Arabia, Japan, Italy, Western European countries, USA	
Foreign debt	US$ 792 million (1981)	
Foreign aid	US$ 149 million, excluding military aid (1981)	
Main natural resources	Gold, manganese ore, quarry salt, platinum	
Food self-sufficiency	Shortage of wheat, teff, barley and pulses since 1977. According to the World Bank (1983) consumption is growing at a 3.4% rate while agricultural production is growing at only a 0.9% rate. Famine due to drought is estimated in 1984 to be affecting 6 million people in the northern regions of Eritrea, Tigre, Beghemdir and Semien, and Wollo, and in the southern region of Sidamo.	

Armed forces	300,000. In 1983 Ethiopia declared all citizens aged 18-30 eligible for conscription, while those aged 30-50 would be considered active reservists if they had previous military training or were retired.
Education and health	
School system	Sixteen years (1980)
Primary school enrolment	43% of school-age children enrolled (1980)
Secondary school enrolment	11% of age group enrolled (1980)
Higher education	1% of age group 20-24 enrolled. Addis Ababa University, University of Asmara (1980)
Adult literacy (%)	17 (1983)
Population per hospital bed	2,857 (1979)
Population per physician	58,490 (1980)
Economy	
GNP	US$ 4.3 billion (1983)
GNP per capita	US$ 120
GDP by %	Agriculture 50, industry 16, services 34 (1981)
State budget (expenditure)	US$ 1 billion (1980)
Defence expenditure % of state budget	33%
Monetary unit	Birr (2.07 birrs equal US$ 1)
Main crops	Coffee (primary crop and major agricultural export), teff, barley, wheat, pulses, oilseeds, livestock
Land tenure	Collectives, and up to 10 hectares usage rights per peasant family unit
Main religions	Ethiopian Orthodox Church, 35-40%; Islam, 40-45%; Animist, 15%; Falasha (Jewish), 0.2%
Transport	
Rail network	1,087 km.
Road network	5,880 km.

Population Forecasting

The following data are projections produced by Poptran, Cardiff University Population Centre, from United Nations Assessment Data published in 1980, and are reproduced here to provide some basis of comparison with other countries covered by the Marxist Regimes Series.

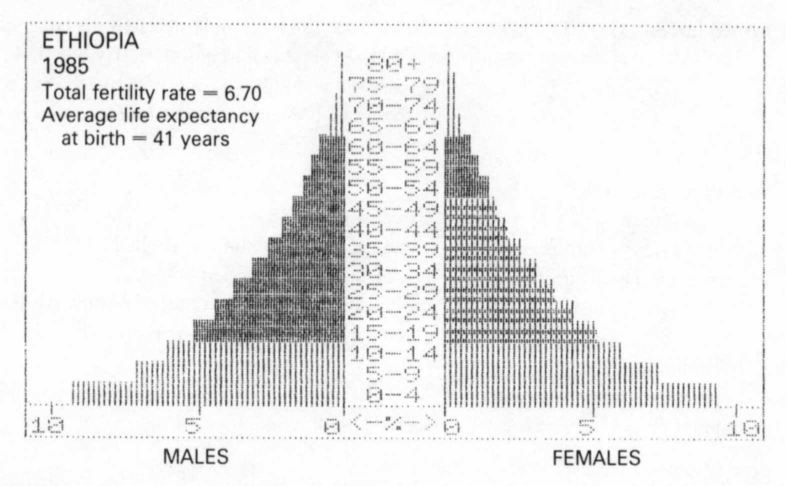

Ethiopia 1985: percentage distribution of population by sex and age projected from data published in 1980

Projected Data for Ethiopia 1985

Total population ('000)	35,627
Males ('000)	17,726
Females ('000)	17,901
Total fertility rate	6.70
Life expectancy (male)	39.5 years
Life expectancy (female)	42.6 years
Crude birth rate	49.7
Crude death rate	23.1
Annual growth rate	2.66%
Under 15s	45.33%
Over 65s	2.51%
Women aged 15-49	22.79%
Doubling time	26 years
Population density	29 per sq. km.
Urban population	17.6%

List of Abbreviations

Note. Two words, that are not abbreviations, are used frequently: Dergue ('Committee'), and Ras ('Prince').

AEPA	All-Ethiopian Peasant Association
AETU	All-Ethiopia Trade Union
ALF	Afar Liberation Front
CELU	Confederation of Ethiopian Labour Unions
CMEA	Council for Mutual Economic Assistance
COPWE	Commission to Organize the Party of the Working People of Ethiopia
DFLE	Democratic Front for the Liberation of Ethiopia
DSPE	Democratic Socialist Part of Ethiopia
EDU	Ethiopian Democratic Union
ELF	Eritrean Liberation Front
ENDRP	Ethiopian National Democratic Revolution Programme
EPDM	Ethiopian People's Democratic Movement
EPDRP	Ethiopian People's Democratic Revolutionary Party
EPLF	Eritrean People's Liberation Front
EPRP	Ethiopian People's Revolutionary Party
EUS	Ethiopian University Service
GATT	General Agreement on Tariffs and Trade
GDP	Gross Domestic Product
GNP	Gross National Product
IMF	International Monetary Fund
NATO	North Atlantic Treaty Organization
OAU	Organization of African Unity
OPEC	Organization of Petroleum Exporting Countries
PEDU	Popular Ethiopian Democratic Union
PMAC	Provisional Military Administrative Committee
POMOA	Provisional Office for Mass Organizational Affairs
REWA	Revolutionary Ethiopia's Women's Association
SDSF	Somali Democratic Salvation Front
TLM	Tigre Liberation Movement
TPLF	Tigre Popular Liberation Front
UN	United Nations

UNECA	United Nations Economic Commission for Africa
UNFAO	United Nations Food and Agriculture Organization
UNICEF	United Nations Children's Fund
US	United States
USSR	Union of Soviet Socialist Republics
WHO	World Health Organization
WP	Workers' Party
WSLF	Western Somali Liberation Front

1 History, Political Traditions and Social Structure

Geographical and Historical Setting

Ethiopia has physical beauty of extraordinary majesty. The roads that are carved on and through the mountains of the north permit vistas that are staggering in their beauty. It is an endless geographical surprise. Astonishing views of the desert, of the Red Sea, of cliffs that fall away from either side of the road, and of the many lovely and lazy lakes that dot the northern countryside are breathtaking. The route north takes one to the gorge of the Blue Nile river, Lake Tana, and into the ancient cities of Gondar and Axum. From there one heads into Eritrea's capital Asmara, a city of boulevards lined with palm trees and Italian architecture. Travelling east one enters the hot, arid region of the Red Sea. The geographical diversity of the highlands is extreme. Moving south-east from Addis Ababa and through the lowlands one passes low rolling mountains, far less rugged than in the north, large lakes often enclosed by sand, and then enters the Ogaden desert. If one travels through Harar there will be seen the ancient walled city, a labyrinth of narrow streets. The city provides a colourful gateway into the Ogaden.

But Ethiopia's landscape is an anomaly within the context of its political tradition. Ethiopian feudalism, the class system it created, the stratification within it, and the vigour with which it was defended by the ruling class and the monarchs rubs against Ethiopia's beauty. Its historical tradition is in contradistinction to its landscape.

Ethiopia, which is located in north-east Africa on a part of the continent known as The Horn, can be divided geographically into the highlands of the north and the lowlands of the south. About two-thirds of the land rises high above the lowlands to form part of the East African Rift Plateau. In Ethiopia its general elevation is 5,000 to 10,000 feet above sea level and it is dotted with high mountain ranges and cratered cones. Erosion has produced steep valleys and rapid waterways. The Great Rift Valley, the earth's most extensive fault, extends from Jordan to

Mozambique. The portion that runs through Ethiopia is marked in the north by the Danakil Depression, a large triangular desert. In some places it is 300 feet below sea level and is one of the hottest places in the world. The north-west region of Ethiopia, around Addis Ababa, is also a rugged plateau but its elevation is slightly lower. To the far north, above the Danakil Depression, is a ten- to fifty-mile wide hot, arid, coastal strip of land which leads to the Red Sea coast. Lake Tana, Ethiopia's largest lake, lies at the centre of the highlands.

In contrast, the lowlands descending from the south-western slopes of the Great Rift Valley are less abrupt and are broken by river exits. This leads to the largely tropical lowland which is sparsely populated. The south-east, in the arid Ogaden, is predominantly semi-desert.

All the country's rivers originate in the highlands and flow outward through gorges. Many are tributaries of the Nile system. The Blue Nile and its tributaries, together with the Tekeze in the north and the Baro in the south, account for half the outflow of water. The eastern part of the highlands is drained by the Omo, while the majestic Awash River flowing north from Addis Ababa disappears into the lakes of the Danakil Depression. In the south-east the Wabi Shebeli courses through Somalia and into the Indian Ocean.

The cool zone in the centre of the western and eastern part of the high plateau has temperatures ranging from 32 to 60 °F. The temperate zone in the high plateau in the north-west has temperatures between 60 and 85 °F, while the hot zone, which encompasses the Danakil Depression, east Ogaden, the lowlands of Eritrea and the belts along the Sudan and Kenya border, has temperatures ranging from 80 to 120 °F.

Vegetation ranges from forests to desert scrub to eucalyptus trees to grasslands. There are minor amounts of gold, manganese ore, quarry salt and platinum. The land area is approximately 54 per cent grassland, 8 per cent is cultivated cropland; forests, which occupy about 7 per cent; while the rest of Ethiopia is desert, water, or non-agricultural land. The many great rivers and streams are not being used to generate hydroelectric power.

Although the country covers 472,000 square miles (1,222,480 sq. km.) much land is underutilized. Coffee is the major export crop; more than 350,000 tons are produced yearly. Teff, a grain used domestically, is planted widely. The livestock population is estimated at 50 million, the largest in Africa. Livestock constitutes about one-eighth of the value of total exports. Industry is basically local and small scale. Transportation is largely by road, but roads are poor and often impassable, and only some 8–9 per cent of the population lives near an all-weather road. Since 1917, there has been a railroad between Addis Ababa and Djibouti used for exporting Ethiopian goods, but the line is often closed because of Ethiopia's constant state of war with Somalia.

Until the revolution of 1974, Ethiopians had little appreciation of the nation, but were orientated towards their ethnic group or the church, particularly the Ethiopian Orthodox Church. Primary reference was certainly not to the state or national government. For most Ethiopians life is difficult and based on primitive techniques of farming. Most rural Ethiopians work very, very hard from early morning until darkness falls, seven days a week. Most farmers do not own oxen, and the men pull their own ploughs aided by their male children. In their mud and wattle huts, village women feed their families, care for their small children, provide all the needs of their household and wait on the male adults and male children. Despite the revolution these traditional and cultural values are difficult to alter. Family life is still stratified along sex lines. The male head of the household is the primary authority figure. In the cities, male authority has been diminished because of Western and Marxist influences, and women play a more powerful family role than they do in rural settings. Religion has also been a factor in reinforcing family role models. Both the Ethiopian Orthodox Church and Islam prohibit the questioning of primary family authority.

Most of Ethiopia's 33.7 million people are peasants who have traditionally made up the lowest strata in the class system. A middle class of urbanized government bureaucrats is small in both numbers and power. No accurate figures can be given for these groups since no census has ever been taken in Ethiopia. All figures are estimated. In 1974 class roles were altered. The lifestyle of the peasants improved somewhat, while the traditional Amhara ruling class was eliminated.

Ethiopia has only one major city—Addis Ababa, the capital, with an estimated population of 1.1 million. Because of the influx of refugees from Eritrea which has been attempting to secede since 1962, the population of Addis Ababa has grown rapidly. Asmara, the once striking and beautiful capital of Eritrea, has been partially destroyed as a result of the secessionist rebellion.

Geographically, Ethiopia is varied and blessed with extreme diversity. It is one of those countries of the world that can be called majestic. Its mountains have afforded a large amount of protection from outside forces and have allowed Ethiopia to develop its social and political system in relative isolation. Largely surrounded by Islam, Christianity has flourished in Ethiopia. Geography has always been a major factor in Ethiopian society.

At the same time Ethiopia has suffered because of geography. Much of the country remains inaccessible and this has hampered any kind of central control. This has produced a situation where local/provincial centres of authority have arisen that have controlled and dominated the local peasantry. The Ethiopian Orthodox Church, individual landlords wielding tremendous authority, and in the north the Islamic church, are three of these centres. Their power has always been reinforced by geography, and by Ethiopia's poverty.

Complementing these centres of authority is the stratification within the family and the reverence for tradition. All together—geography, local authority, tradition, and a triangular model of family authority—have made any kind of change very difficult to bring about, even granting that forces existed in the past that wanted such change (see Levine, 1965 for more on this subject). All have had a bearing on the history and society of Ethiopia.

The history of Ethiopia stretches over more than three thousand years. During that time great empires such as Axum and important emperors such as Melenik II (1889–1913) and Haile Selassie I (1930–74) played an important role in the evolution of the country.

Once known as Abyssinia, Ethiopia is mentioned by both Homer and Herodotus and is also referred to in the Old Testament. The Semitic settlers of original Ethiopia arrived from Arabia in the first half of the first millennium BC, mixed with local Cushites, eventually organized themselves into the kingdom of Axum, and became a dominant power in the Red Sea region. During the fourth century AD these forebears of the people of Tigre were converted to Christianity, and Ezana, King of Axum, proclaimed fealty to the Coptic Christian Church of Egypt that adhered to the doctrine of Monophysitism, i.e. the belief that the human and divine in Christ constitute only one nature. The new religion, which became institutionalized in the Ethiopian Orthodox Church, evolved into an indigenous political and economic power that all future emperors had to reckon with.

Until the seventh century when it came into conflict with Islam, Axum flourished and expanded.

The Agau dynasty appeared during the period around 1137 and occupied the throne for a century. Its claim was contested by a group based in Shoa-Amhara province and tracing itself to King Solomon; in 1270 it established the Solomonic dynasty and proclaimed the Amhara region the political centre of the state. Throughout the following centuries the new dynasty spread its power and influence into the south and south-east sections of the plateau and consistently and often unsuccessfully battled incursions into its territory first by Muslim forces, and then by the Oromo. After the sixteenth-century defeat of the Muslims, who were intent on destroying the Christian stronghold, the Oromo overran the territories of the south and south-east. Not until the nineteenth century were the Oromo incorporated into the dominion of the Shoa. During the reign of Sahle Selassie (1813–47), Shoa took the south, west, and south-eastern territories and the king proclaimed himself ruler of Shoa and of the Oromo. Ethiopia enlarged its territory during the next fifty years under the dominance of emperors Theodore II, Yohannes IV and Menelik II of Shoa. It was during the reign of Menelik II that the empire was virtually doubled in size, leading to the creation of boundaries that have lasted, more or less, until today. Thus, Ethiopia is the only state south of the Sahara that utilized classic techniques of imperialism and expansion through military conquest to determine its geographical boundaries. It is therefore distinctive within Africa where all other states south of the Sahara have had their geographical limits established by European colonial powers. To those forces within Ethiopia who presently question the sanctity of the state this issue is fundamental.

The most dramatic and enduring myth had been utilized by the Solomonic dynasty to legitimate its rule: it is said that Sheba, Queen of Ethiopia, visited Solomon, King of Jerusalem, converted to Judaism and bore Solomon a son, Menelik I. The son later travelled from Ethiopia to Jerusalem to see his father whereupon he stole the ark of the covenant and returned home with it. Menelik I was considered related to Christ through the holy man Solomon, since the latter two were seen as the personification of God's will on earth, and the Solomonic line of Ethiopian kings claimed the inheritance of the theology upon Christ's rejection by the Jews and became a Christian dynasty. Christianity and the mythical birth of

Menelik I were considered the roots of the Solomonic dynasty in Ethiopia, both being utilized to legitimize its divine right to the throne. Both the 1931 and 1955 constitutions translated this myth into legality and thus its importance and vitality to the House of Solomon cannot be underrated. The myth was also used to draw the multiple peoples of Ethiopia together. The populace of the country consists of two main groups, Cushite and Semitic. The latter and elements of the former entered the area from Arabia. The Cushites include the Agau, Falasha (Ethiopian Jews), the Sidama of the south-west (which includes Sidamo, Wolamo, and Kaffa peoples), the Afar, Saho and Somalis. The Gallinya-speaking Oromo are the largest ethnic group of Cushite peoples. The Semites consist of Amhara centred in Shoa region, and Tigrai, while a smaller group, known as the Shankella, are linked with the Nilotic peoples of southern Sudan. Tigrinya, developed from the traditional and ancient Ge'es language, is widely spoken in the north, as is Arabic. While Amharic has been the culturally predominant language, English and Italian are also spoken in government and bureaucratic circles.

Historically, the country has been dominated by the Shoan-Amhara who, together with other Amhara and the Tigrai, constitute about one-third of the population and inhabit the northern provinces. Both the Amhara and Tigrai are Ethiopian Orthodox Christians. The largest ethnic group in Ethiopia, the Oromo, are bound by a common language and live in the south. Those that reside close to the Muslim population in the east have adopted Islam as their own religion while those living in the south-west have joined the Ethiopian Orthodox Church. Although the Amhara and Tigrai are a minority of the population they have been the politically dominant force in the country. The Amharic culture was almost always the primary standard imposed whenever and wherever possible on all other ethnic and religious groups. The Amhara, and to a limited extent the Tigrai, were until 1974 in fundamental control of the political, economic, social and religious system.

The Ethiopian Orthodox Church was, until the overthrow of Haile Selassie I in 1974, the established church of the empire and its hierarchy is made up almost entirely of Amhara-Tigrai. Some 35 per cent of the population are adherents to this theology, while some 45 per cent of the population are Muslims. A much smaller number of peoples are practitioners of animism, and a tiny Jewish group known as the Falasha reside around the town of Gondar.

So, despite the fact that Ethiopia is extraordinarily diverse in culture with a broad mix of ethnic groups and religions, the Amhara and the Christian Church have for centuries together controlled the political culture of the country. They acted in unison to foster a policy of imperialism incorporating vast chunks of territory into the realm, and in so far as they were able, they prevented any other group from attaining power. Domestically they brought the Muslims, Oromo, Sidama, Arusi and Somali under their heel, and internationally they prevented other countries from establishing suzerainty over Ethiopia. The Turks, Portuguese, Egyptians, and (under Menelik and Haile Selassie) the Italians were all defeated in their attempts to establish themselves.

Feudalism in Ethiopia was the bedrock of the entire political and social system. Without the feudal structure the Shoa-Amhara would never have been able to control Ethiopia as long as they did (Hoben, 1973; Schwab, 1972; Gilkes, 1975). Status, class and power were shaped by it and the political order was based upon it. The ruling class of contemporary Ethiopia was made up essentially of individuals who were responsible to or supportive of Haile Selassie I. As the great warlords of the nineteenth century died off, Haile Selassie appointed his supporters to positions in the central or local administration. Many were given large quantities of land as patronage and many were already large landowners. These landlords and government officials, together with the Ethiopian Orthodox Church, owned the bulk of the land in the country and controlled the everyday lives of the peasantry. This landed class imposed upon an oppressed class of tenant farmers a power hold in which the latter held no legal, political or economic rights. Prior to Haile Selassie a feudal nobility also controlled the lives of peasants. In the nineteenth century, for example, Ras Makonnen, Haile Selassie's father,

> patterned his house along the lines demanded of an Amharic nobleman. With a personal military of more than six thousand men, and owning a huge amount of tax-free land partly inherited and partly bestowed upon him by Menelik, *Ras* Makonnen was a classic example of the old nobility who represented the pinnacle of status and class in Ethiopia. The Makonnen house was based upon the model established in the imperial court . . . Masses of retainers and servants met the personal needs of all members of the family; the army was used to ensure the payment of rent

and taxes by tenant farmers and to secure the property from the armies of other noblemen . . . [Schwab, 1979, p. 25]

But through tax and land tenure legislation initiated by Haile Selassie the feudal system was legitimized within the political structure.

The Ethiopian Orthodox Church is one of the most reactionary and was one of the most powerful institutions in the country. Church ownership of land was rooted in the traditional right of emperors to grant lands to churches and monasteries that included tax privileges, a right going back to biblical times. Prior to 1974 the Church owned some 18 per cent of the land in the country. Legally and traditionally exempt from the payment of land taxes, the Church, in 1942, was granted the statutory right to collect its own private taxes from its tenants, something it had always traditionally done in any case. Through tax collection, tax exemption and rental of land, the Church evolved into a political, social and economic power of unusually large dimensions.

Most of the land outside the provinces of Gojjam, Tigre and Beghemdir/Semien, where land is held communally, was owned by individual landlords, many who at one time or another held government positions and who maintained a rigid feudal relationship to tenant farmers. Through traditional and contemporary tax exemptions they remained almost totally free of land tax obligations, while at the same time they too were granted rights to tax their tenants privately and mercilessly. Traditional tax exemptions were often tied to individual rights to collect taxes. Under the *rist-gult* form of land tenure, granted since the Middle Ages by emperors to members of the royal family for services rendered, the landowner was entitled to collect and keep taxes under prescribed rates. *Maderia* land, granted to individuals in place of salary, was exempt from land tax, as was *Galla* land which was granted to landlords as pension. *Woqf* lands, granted to the Islamic Church, were also exempt from land taxes. (See Schwab, 1972, pp. 27–86.)

When land tenure did not call for exemptions landlords often illegally shifted the burden of payment of land taxes upon the tenant farmer. And since the tenant farmer held no functional legal rights, refusal to pay meant eviction. In addition, landlords demanded at least 50 per cent of the produce as rent, loaned money to tenant farmers at above 100 per cent interest rates, demanded free services such as threshing, fencing, and herding of cattle, and collected a 10 per cent tithe on produce (a traditional practice in Ethiopia since earliest times).

Under Haile Selassie, the Church, the Imperial family (which itself owned some 42 per cent of the total land in the state) and the landed class made up a polity, that to some degree competed structurally. The Church and the landed class were competing entities absorbing whatever surplus income was extracted from the land. The Imperial Office and the individuals who filled positions in the politically impotent parliament were also property owners free from land taxes and able to tax tenants. To function financially the government had to compete with the Church, the Imperial household and landlords in terms of taxation. Therefore the tenant farmer was seen as the only taxable entity in a political system made up of an oppressor class unwilling to make any financial sacrifices. Compelling evidence of the ability of the ruling class to withhold government revenues is indicated by the fact that in 1966/7, revenue from land taxes and tithe totalled less than 4 per cent of total government revenues. This is despite the fact that the Ethiopian economy is a basically rural economy in which agriculture employs over 80 per cent of the total population (Bequele & Chole, 1969, p. 28; *Ethiopia Statistical Abstract*, 1966, p. 147).

The peasant, prior to and under the regime of Haile Selassie, bore the brunt of supporting four layers of the political and social system: the landed elite, the Church, the central government and the Imperial family. In this structure the peasant easily fits under the rubric of serf. Oppressed without mercy, he was lucky to survive from year to year. No leader ever came close to altering the feudal structure until 1974, and in fact emperors usually supported it, since it was the determining factor in the accumulation of class and power. Tinkering with feudalism was seen as treasonable and would promptly bring about unified opposition among the traditional forces whose power was seen as threatened. As in the case of Theodore II (1855–68) who tried to curtail the Church's land tax rights, it could even lead to the overthrow of an emperor. Feudalism was without question the political and economic context within which all emperors had to operate if they wanted to survive, for the conservative forces in the country would not tolerate the reform of a system upon which their power was based.

Because of its direct access to the Red Sea, Ethiopia has been viewed by the superpowers as strategically and geopolitically important, particularly as regards shipment of oil from Persian Gulf states to Western Europe and the United States. Thus, both the United States and the Soviet Union have viewed Ethiopia as geographically central to their own national interests. This is clearly indicated by the extensive support both states have given Ethiopia at different times. Between 1953 and 1970, half of all United States military aid to Africa was sent to Ethiopia and the amount of military aid during this period totalled $305 million (*US Security Agreements*, 1970, p. 1888). Since 1977 more than $3,000 million in military aid has been sent by the Soviet Union to Ethiopia (1982, 1983 *Yearbook on International Communist Affairs*). Ethiopia has traditionally used both superpowers to support its own national interests. In 1948 the Ogaden was incorporated into the empire, to the dismay of Somalia (which received its independence on 1 July 1960), which had historically considered the Ogaden culturally and politically part of its own territory. In 1962, Eritrea, the former Italian colony, was absorbed into Ethiopia through the shady but deft political manœuvres of Haile Selassie (see Sherman, 1980). In addition to pursuing an imperial policy established by previous emperors, Haile Selassie considered Eritrea vital to Ethiopia's interest because of Eritrea's position on the Red Sea. Without Eritrea, Ethiopia is land-locked. The two primary ports of Massawa and Assab, located in Eritrea, provided Ethiopia with outlets directly on the Red Sea. In the period after 1977 Soviet and Cuban aid and military force was instrumental in defeating Somalia's invasion of the Ogaden, and in the virtual destruction of the secessionist forces in Eritrea. Although the United States and the Soviet Union benefited from their relationship to Ethiopia, both directly and indirectly, Ethiopia too gained greatly from its superpower connections. It gained the support to both expand and defend its territory, and it acquired the monetary support to gain time to attempt to stabilize and legitimize its various governments. Both Haile Selassie and Mengistu Haile Mariam were skilful in using the superpowers to further their own as well as Ethiopia's interests (see Ottaway, 1982).

Emperor Haile Selassie was almost synonymous with contemporary Ethiopia, but his overthrow in 1974 and his death one year later (under mysterious circumstances but said to be due to the after-effects of a prostate gland operation) marked the end of an era of absolutism. Ruling Ethiopia like a medieval autocrat, he was for almost the entire span of his leadership the most powerful and dominant politician in the country. He was haughty and regal, in control of all decision-making, and at the pinnacle of an imperial palace structure so patrimonial that all others in the system, including his family, were regarded by Haile Selassie as retainers. Through a combination of charisma, patrimony and feudalism, Haile Selassie maintained his imperial authority. He apparently believed that his authority was bestowed upon him by God and that the positive qualities of all previous emperors had been transmitted to him by biological descent and by the act of consecration in which he was annointed head of the Ethiopian Orthodox Church. Almost all in the executive office or Imperial Palace had to consistently court his favour by daily appearing at the palace, fawning over him, and doing his bidding. One might lose power and authority by not showing proper fealty or by appearing too independent. Through a feudal system of land ownership, distribution and land taxation (see Figure 1), Haile Selassie prevented any mass opposition.

Until 1974 this charismatic, patrimonial, feudal system with Haile Selassie on top of it held together. The emperor was such an overwhelming figure inside and out of Ethiopia that it came as a complete surprise when he was deposed by the Dergue. In retrospect, it should not have been so shocking, for the events leading to the removal of this feudal system were set in motion a decade earlier. Grumbling and opposition to the regime evolved in 1967 into an acute political rebellion that set the stage for the development of a radical and socialist Ethiopia.

The Collapse of the Feudal Autocracy

Since 1960, when an abortive coup against Haile Selassie took place, led by elements of the Imperial Guard, the Ethiopian military has recognized its political power. To keep the armed forces in line, pay increases were granted by the emperor in 1961; these had previously been rejected as an unnecessary financial burden. In 1965, in a further effort to develop the support of the military, serving members of the armed forces were granted tax-free title to forty hectares of land each. Using traditional sources of patronage, Haile Selassie had tried to introduce a modern military system in an archaic and feudal Ethiopia. His actions, however, had the opposite effect. By 1965 the political consciousness of junior

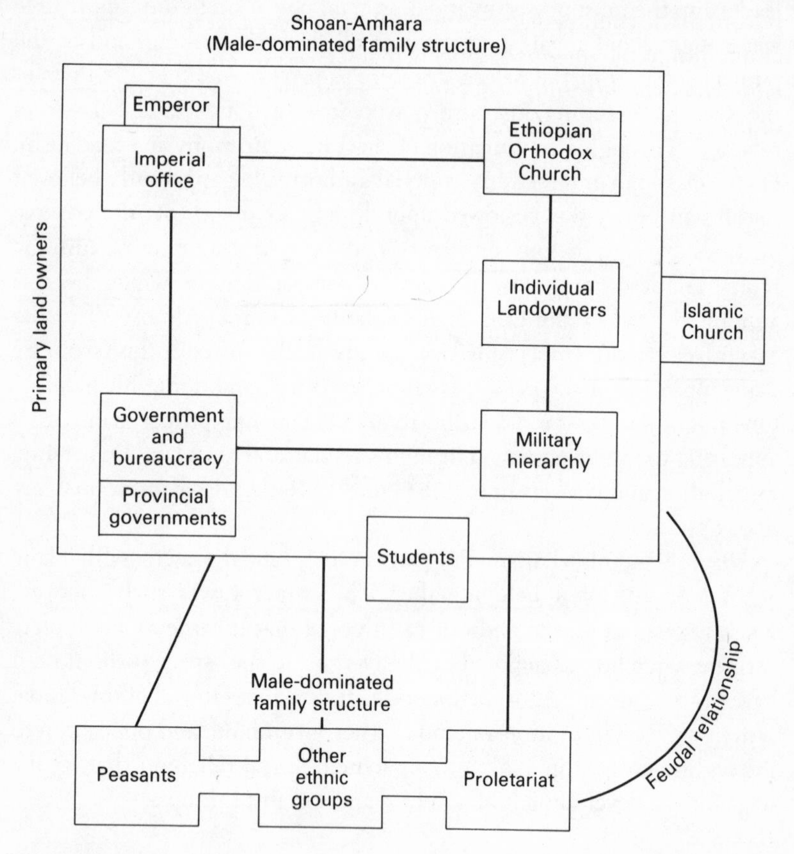

Figure 1. Feudal Ethiopia: The Social/Political Structure

officers had increased considerably. They realized that in 1960 the armed forces had been the only entity able to prevent the overthrow of Haile Selassie and now began generating demands. The military was no longer apolitical and was not prepared to do the emperor's bidding unless he met their expectations. Haile Selassie, by advancing financial benefits to the military, assumed it could be bought off so that it would not question a regime which after 1960 was kept in power by its guns.The techniques of control, honed and developed through the years to garner the allegiance of the myriad political sectors of Ethiopia, no longer operated with precision. For Haile Selassie, in gaining the support of the military in the slow reform of the country, had created a political force that tried to coerce the emperor into moving more quickly than he was willing to. After 1960 his authority over the military declined as it saw that the political legitimacy of the emperor's regime was non-existent.

Independent political consciousness was also developed within the military in respect of both the Eritrean conflict (under way since 1962) and the 1967–8 Gojjam rebellion. With half the army stationed in Eritrea, opposing the secessionist liberation armies, and with some one thousand troops utilized to halt the Gojjam rebellion, the military became aware that it was not only defending the political structure but the entire feudal fabric of Ethiopia. Its political education was reinforced by these events.

Gojjam, which rebelled against a 1967 land reform programme using both political and military tactics, took on vast political overtones. (See Schwab, 1972, ch. 8 for a discussion of the Gojjam revolt.) It clearly pointed out the stunning weakness of imperial authority. If Gojjam was such a threat, then the revolutionary situation posed by the Eritrean rebels was far more politically dangerous to the regime and its ideology than had previously been recognized. The 1960 coup suggested the possibility of a student, intellectual, military, peasant front in opposition to the feudal system. Gojjam showed the weakness of the government in dealing with non-revolutionary violence of a feudal nature. The inability of the Haile Selassie government to stem the movement of the ever more powerful and successful liberation fighters in Eritrea showed clearly the regime's political weakness in halting revolutionary violence. Together, the 1960 abortive coup, Gojjam and Eritrea, showed the contradictions inherent in the ruling class and its inability to deal with violently articulated opposition. This lesson was not lost on the military.

Students too became politicized during this period. A growing number of them have been involved in political activity since 1960. With the stymied coup as the starting point, many students at Haile Selassie I University (renamed Addis Ababa University in 1975) have since 1967 articulated their growing class consciousness. Students pressured for land reform in 1967, 1968 and 1974, and for political reform within the university in 1968, 1969 and 1970. In 1972, after repeated protests by students against high-school leaving examinations seen as limiting college entrance, government troops and police stormed the university campus in Addis Ababa and some two thousand students were arrested and expelled. The students were rebelling against Haile Selassie whom they accused of moving too slowly in political reforms. Both they, and elements of the military, had moved far ahead of the emperor politically.

Though largely reformist, the students represented a link among three groups: the younger military officers who opposed the feudal state, had the guns, and were not tied directly to the aristocracy; the urban proletariat, which became more and more outspoken in its discontent; and the peasants. Through the Ethiopian University Service (EUS), in which the third year of university was spent in the interior teaching or aiding in agricultural development, the students had the ability to communicate their discontent to the peasants. Thus the 1960 abortive coup, Gojjam, Eritrea and the violence against students were essential factors that tied together opposition to the feudal Ethiopian regime into a loose political community. In 1974 this community became firmly intertwined and destroyed the government of Haile Selassie.

On three crucial occasions, in 1960, in 1967/8 in Gojjam, and in 1974 when Haile Selassie was finally overthrown, the emperor's authority, based on the shifting sand of charisma, tradition and feudalism, was not adequate to maintain the loyalty of significant groups within the population. His longstanding ability to reconcile competing interests within the context of reform failed largely because reform was not possible given the feudal nature of the state.

In 1973, however, the concern of the population, of all classes, was directed to a spreading drought. Afraid that the image of Ethiopia would be tarnished if world publicity were directed at Ethiopia's inability to feed its stricken population, Haile Selassie refused to allow international relief organizations to come to Ethiopia's aid. As a result, the relief organizations, in order to maintain proper diplomatic relations with Ethiopia remained silent and went along with Ethiopia's cover-up of the famine (see Shepherd, 1975). Since Haile Selassie 'didn't wish [Ethiopia] to appear "just another Sahel" . . . [and] believed drought and famine "normal" for Ethiopia' (ibid., p. ix) the cover-up was instituted. As one of the emperor's palace retainers explained:

> First of all death from hunger had existed in our Empire for hundreds of years, an everyday, natural thing, and it never occurred to anyone to make any noise about it. Drought would come and the earth would dry up, the cattle would drop dead, the peasants would starve. Ordinary, in accordance with the laws of nature and the eternal

order of things . . . Consider also . . . that it is not bad for national order and a sense of national humility that the subjects be rendered skinnier, thinned down a bit. [Kapuscinski, 1983, pp. 111, 112.]

And how did the emperor respond to all the suffering and misery? 'For the starvelings it had to suffice that His Munificent Highness personally attached the greatest importance to their fate, which was a very special kind of attachment, of an order higher than the highest. It provided the subjects with a soothing and uplifting hope . . .' (ibid., p. 119). No food, no aid, merely an uplifting hope! And when some relief supplies did finally reach Ethiopia further scandalous activity took place: ministers first demanded customs fees from overseas donors and then appropriated the food shipments, and then sold them to those who could afford to buy.

The politics of the whole outrage is best summed up by Haile Selassie's retainer: 'The usefulness of going hungry is that a hungry man thinks only of bread. He's all wrapped up in the thought of food' (ibid., p. 113).

With the emperor and the government refusing to take any responsibility for dealing with the crisis, drought spread to famine and some 300,000 people in eleven regions died. According to a 1974 UN Food and Agriculture Organization report, 2 million Ethiopians were made destitute by the famine between 1973 and 1974. Whole villages and districts were deserted while life was shattered; in some areas there was nothing left for Ethiopian peasants to return to. The drought and famine was an economic catastrophe that became Haile Selassie's political coffin. Only in November 1973, some eleven months after the drought began, did the emperor permit relief supplies into Ethiopia. Only then did it leak out to an astounded world that organizations such as the World Health Organization (WHO) and the United Nations Children's Emergency Fund (UNICEF) had participated with Haile Selassie in covering up the tragedy. Dissatisfaction and anger among the military, among the peasantry, among the students and the urban middle class fed the so-called 'creeping coup' that began in February 1974 and by September of that year had led to the abolition of the monarchy. The proportions of the tragedy, unknown to the world, were evident within Ethiopia as thousands of peasants made their way to the cities for relief. Permitting hundreds of thousands to die merely so that Ethiopia could save face was a cynical act and political blunder that led virtually an entire population, left, centre, and right, to question the leadership of the emperor.

By February 1974 when Haile Selassie had made the first public pronouncements on the famine, the monarchy and the entire feudal system was already disintegrating. Whatever support and legitimacy the government had was swept away in 1974, and to a very large degree the cover-up of the famine was directly related to the dissolution of the regime. One other element which significantly contributed to this process was the international oil crisis, which brought about increased inflation and economic pressure on all except the upper class in the country. These two events, the famine and the oil crisis, impinged upon Ethiopia, and led to increasing opposition to economic and political decisions.

Pointedly however, the struggle that ensued as a result of the political débâcle surrounding the famine and that led to the overthrow of the monarchy, might not have come about were it not for the heightened political consciousness of the military and students that occurred in the decade of the 1960s. Had the emperor been able to use his traditionally successful techniques that flowed from patrimony and feudalism, he would probably have been able to survive the disenchantment that arose in 1973 and 1974. However, the unprecedented politicization of the students and certain elements of the military enabled these two groups to place the famine and the oil crisis into a political framework that consequently allowed them both an understanding of their political position and the comprehension that they were opposing a feudal autocracy that would permit almost no reform of the system. They became increasingly conscious, on the basis of the experience of previous decades, that to alter the system or any of its fundamental components meant a challenge to or even the destruction of the system itself.

It all began in February 1974. In the wake of civil disturbances reflecting public concern over increasing prices, soaring inflation, unemployment and the spreading famine dissident military forces took over a number of Ethiopian cities and surrounded all public buildings in Addis Ababa. Calling for military pay increases, land reform programmes, and the dismissal of the cabinet, junior officers who organized the revolt forced the emperor to submit to all their demands by March. During these very same months, strikes—an unheard-of phenomenon in Ethiopia—took place throughout the country. With the support of the military rebels, the strikers' demands for higher wages were granted by Haile Selassie. The newly appointed Prime Minister, Endalkachew

Makonnen, a member of the Ethiopian aristocracy, appointed a new cabinet, promising to embark on a large-scale land reform programme that would eliminate the worst element of the feudal land system. Former Prime Minister Aklilu Habte Wold and many in his cabinet were placed under arrest on charges of corruption and self-enrichment at public expense. But the rebel leaders were not satisfied with the new government, in particular because of its refusal to implement the promised land reform. Pressure was increased by the junior officers and the emperor dismissed the lord mayor of Addis Ababa, the deputy military chief of staff, and a number of regional governors-general. Haile Selassie had tried to use a reform element within the aristocracy to still the opposition, apparently believing that the radicals were reformers and would accept the political crumbs he was offering. But he was unable to quell the growing military and civilian upheavals.

Through the efforts of Foreign Minister Zewde Gebre-Selassie a constitutional convention was called to formulate a constitution incorporating the demanded political reforms. This included naming a successor to the throne—the emperor's 21-year old grandson Prince Zara Yacob, son of the invalid Crown Prince Asfa Wossen. Given the history of the Crown Prince's stormy relationship with his father Haile Selassie, Asfa Wossen's removal from the line of succession was to be expected (Schwab, 1979, ch. 11). The prince, however, refused to return to Ethiopia from England, and this aspect of the proposed new constitution was still-born. The belatedness and irony of this move, however, is that for years Haile Selassie had ignored 'the advice of virtually all his closest advisers, including the chairman of the Crown Council, *Ras* Asrate Kassa, and his Prime Minister, Aklilu Habte Wold, who had been urging on him for at least three years that he should make way . . . for an orderly succession through his son . . . and his grandson' (Legum, 1975, p. 30).

The 120-man Dergue (the newly organized Coordinating Committee of the Armed Forces, Police and the Territorial Army formed to direct the opposition to the emperor) felt the emperor was dragging his feet and at the same time trying to organize opposition to the Dergue through the new government of Endalkachew Makonnen. In July, when it became clear that the Constitutional Convention was largely irrelevant, scores of government officials were rounded up and arrested. Among those arrested by the Dergue were some of the most important politicians in

Ethiopia. They included Ras Asrate Kassa; former Minister of Finance Yilma Deressa; Minasse Haile, former Minister of Foreign Affairs; the Minister of Defence, General Abiye Abebe; Iskander Desta, the emperor's grandson; Endalkachew Makonnen; and Abebe Retta, the Keeper of the Royal Privy Purse. The military dissidents then insisted of Haile Selassie that political and social reforms proceed rapidly.

Endalkachew Makonnen, a wealthy landowner and a believer in the feudal system had, as prime minister, tried to appease the Dergue via the rhetoric of change but proceeded at a snail's pace to implement any reforms, doing what he could to hamper the movement towards reform. In the first months of 1974, when junior officers made explicit demands and the emperor was meeting these demands in limited fashion, the traditionals in Ethiopia fought every step of the way, despite the possible consequences of a direct military takeover. Haile Selassie was caught in an impossible political bind. His authority over the military, weak since 1960, forced him to agree to its demands; this in turn weakened his authority over traditional conservative allies who themselves tried to disrupt the reform movement of the Dergue. The dilemma faced by Haile Selassie in 1967 in Gojjam confronted him again in 1974:

> [The government in its effort] to break down tradition [has] alerted the forces representing tradition who see the threat to their political existence, and have therefore prepared politically and physically to combat institutional application of modern legislation. So too, however, have the forces representing modernization been alerted; forces who feel the Emperor is not moving quickly enough in bringing about change. Thus, the interests both of the traditional sector and the modernizing sector raise pressures impossible for the government to accommodate, and which are likely to be increasingly difficult to maintain with the political system now in existence ... [Schwab, 1972, p.182.]

By September 1974 more than 250 Ethiopian leaders were imprisoned in the basement of the Imperial Grand Palace; others were placed in Akaki prison in the centre of Addis Ababa where many of the emperor's family were also incarcerated. By this time virtually all Haile Selassie's associates and palace retainers were under arrest. Michael Imru, a reformist liberal representative of the Shoan aristocracy was appointed prime minister and energetically tried to implement the land reform insisted upon by the Dergue. In early August, he announced that a draft constitution had been completed. The draft would make the emperor a constitutional monarch, severely limit his powers, and give increased authority, including the right to select a prime minister, to an elected parliament. But the Dergue was not impressed. At this time one of its prominent members was Lt.-Col. Mengistu Haile Mariam, a Shankella radicalized by a class awareness that was reinforced by a short educational training programme at the University of Maryland. Two of its close advisers were Lt.-Gen. Aman Michael Andom, an Eritrean who as a young boy returned with Haile Selassie to Ethiopia from Sudan where his family had been in exile during the Italian occupation, and Brig.-Gen. Teferi Banti, a Shoan who served for a time as military attaché in Washington, D.C. The Dergue was furious that Haile Selassie seemed to be using constitutional structures to bury the demands of the military in a bureaucratic pit.

At this point decision-making within the Dergue was democratically organized and consisted of committees within each military unit composed of privates, non-commissioned officers and junior officers. Meetings were held on a regular basis. Each of the forty units of the army and police sent three members to the Dergue, which made decisions which reflected the desires of the various military units.

The Dergue, in effective political control of Ethiopia, was now faced with the issue of what to do about Haile Selassie, a man of international stature who in fact led a government that brutalized its own peasant population. To the Dergue it was clear that (1) Haile Selassie was still trying to limit the implementation of its demands; (2) he was powerless and totally isolated, and perhaps most importantly (3) it both wanted and was now in a position to take control of the levers of power. Some liberals in the Dergue however argued for a constitutional monarchy based upon the European model. 'With their identity purposely kept publicly unknown, but supported almost totally by the rank and file of the military, the members of the Dergue argued fiercely among themselves': was it to be a constitutional monarchy, or a radical restructuring of the social and political system? (Schwab, 1981, p. 298.) Toward the end of August a decision had been made. The palaces were nationalized, the Crown Council, the emperor's Chilot (court), and the Imperial Court were abolished. The extent of Haile Selassie's personal corruption was publicized and his private wealth was exposed for the first time.

During the week of 5 September the Dergue prepared the population for the final act.

> Posters appeared in the capital which juxtaposed photographs of horribly emaciated famine victims with others showing the Emperor . . . feeding his dogs with choice cuts of meat. At a subsequent demonstration in the capital, his deposal and execution were demanded. The night before the final act [a] film on the famine was shown on television, followed by filmed scenes of imperial extravagance, including sumptuous state dinners . . . [Markakis & Ayele, 1978, p. 113.]

On 12 September 1974 parliament was dissolved and Haile Selassie was deposed and arrested. The Dergue had approached the politically stultifying social system by eliminating the old political and social structures rather than modifying them. With the breakup of the old political order, a new radical social order would be created. With his arrest late in the day the public persona of the emperor came to a close. Little is known about how the emperor spent his final year under palace arrest. The Dergue, fearing that Haile Selassie could be used by its opponents as a rallying point, issued no information on his activities. After being moved from one palace to another he finally died on 27 August 1975. He was buried quickly and secretly.

Now that Haile Selassie and the political system that he fashioned had been eliminated, the Dergue would set about organizing a social system based on socialist values. In fact it moved very quickly to implement many of the changes it had been urging the emperor to adopt. Rather than changing society within the old rules of the game, it adopted new ones. Yet the road toward a socialist Ethiopia would not be easy to travel because of continued fierce arguments within the Dergue, and between the Dergue and the civilian left in Ethiopia. The radical elements within the Dergue were confronted with opposition from 1974 to 1978, making the implementation of socialism from above a stormy and violent process. With the removal of Haile Selassie the first truly revolutionary act had been instituted. What followed was a turbulent and in some ways murderous revolution, that would within little more than half a decade begin to stabilize and organize itself under the auspices of the radical elements of the Dergue led by Mengistu Haile Mariam. The Ethiopian revolution has been called 'the most profound African revolution in contemporary African history' (Halliday & Molyneux, 1981, p. 266). In addition it has been argued that this revolution is a true model, in that military officers were seen as capable of playing a vanguard role in the creation and establishment of socialism (ibid., p. 275). The revolution was uncompromising on its path towards socialism and left in its wake those of the right, left and centre who could not abide the violence which it thought necessary to replace feudalism with socialism. The feudal and class struggle evoked by the revolution provided many victims. But the Dergue's analysis of the struggle was apparently correct as the revolution moved to secure economic redistribution to the peasants of Ethiopia. Capitalism and liberalism were rejected while socialism, and further on communism, became the goal of the revolutionaries. In 1974, then, a group of revolutionary officers began to lead Ethiopian society in a socialist direction.

The Dergue Takes Power

The Dergue, whose membership at this time was generally unknown, created a Provisional Military Administrative Committee (PMAC) to take over control of the government apparatus. Since the Dergue was based on the concept of democratic decision-making it seemed necessary to create a separate entity to avoid power disputes among its members. PMAC, however, failed to prevent the emergence of ideological disputes and became merely a label the Dergue used to deflect attention away from itself. The first two chairmen of PMAC were purposely chosen from outside the Dergue–Aman Michael Andom and Teferi Banti. Both however became embroiled in the political disputes surrounding the Dergue and both were executed as a result of their political positions. Michael Imru, the deposed prime minister, became political adviser to the Dergue. From September 1974 to February 1977, class and power disputes swirled around the Dergue. Foremost among the issues to be resolved were: (1) Would the graduates of the military academy at Harar or of the Guenet Military School in Holeta dominate? The former, primarily from landowning families, were largely Amhara, and represented a liberal political view that was Western in approach. The Holeta graduates represented a far more radical approach, tended to be lower ranking junior officers and were not of the aristocracy. Mengistu Haile Mariam, who emerged in 1977 as the absolute and primary leader of the Dergue, was a Holeta graduate. (2) Would the new Ethiopia move sharply left, or would it attempt to adhere to a centrist, more Western approach? (3) Should there be negotiations with the Eritrean liberation movements as advocated by Andom or should Haile Selassie's policy of militarily opposing the secessionists be maintained? (4) Should Ethiopia seek to continue and expand its ties to the United States or should it try to expand its interests more in the direction of the Soviet Union and the Soviet bloc countries? Paul Brietzke has summarized the operation of the Dergue at this time as follows (1982, pp. 149–50):

> The Dergue . . . was hastily created, with blurred lines of authority. . . . The potential for violent conflict . . . a maximum. . . . While few members . . . are wholly committed Marxists . . . several . . . have pronounced leftward leanings. . . . Senior officers were excluded . . . on the grounds that they would intimidate more junior members. . . . The major policy conflicts revolved around the timetable for a return to civilian government, whether policies of reconciliation or repression should be adopted for Eritrea, the treatment of traditional elites, and the nature of projected land reforms and changes in local administration.

Basically then, the Dergue took control of Ethiopia, directed economic, political and social change, but was for more than two years engulfed in its own class struggle. On the basis of this struggle 'a process of radicalization and post-revolutionary consolidation [took place], through which the PMAC established a stable new order on the ruins of the old' (Halliday & Molyneux, 1981, p. 96).

It also became evident that the Dergue would have only limited support from the left in Ethiopia. The Ethiopian People's Revolutionary Party (EPRP), organized in 1974 as a 'proletarian party' and composed of urban intellectuals and college and secondary-school students, maintained that a Marxist revolution could not be directed through a military regime and that class contradictions could only be provoked through a mass people's revolution. Seeing itself as Maoist the EPRP refused to support the Dergue and in fact confronted the Dergue and opposed virtually all its policies.

Thus, when the Dergue took power in 1974 it was confronted with its own class contradictions, and with public and political opposition from the right and the left.

> The pattern of revolutionary transformation seemed to involve a deep paradox, namely the conflict between the military leadership at the top and the various radical civilian forces below. . . . Indeed [the Dergue] put into practice much of what the civilians were themselves demanding. But no stable alliance between them proved possible. . . . The revolutionary transformation effected by the PMAC therefore involved both the

implementation of a radical social programme and the destruction or at least submission of other forces that helped to bring these changes about. [Ibid.]

The Ethiopian situation thus evolved from 'a people's revolution, a mass spontaneous revolution, to one where the armed forces gave direction in the absence of a revolutionary party or movement' (Vivo, 1978, p. 61). The class warfare that occurred within and outside of the Dergue is 'one of the reasons why the Ethiopian Revolution had a sharp concept of the class struggle and possibly why it developed into one of the fiercest class battles in all the African continent' (José Pérez Novoa, as quoted in ibid., p. 63).

When the Dergue took power the bitter ideological struggle that ensued was initially kept within the framework of discussion. Later it inexorably moved to the level of violence and bloodshed. By early 1975

the liberals within the Dergue . . . had lost out to the self-professed Marxists. But the bloodshed continued as Marxists violently disputed among themselves how best to attain a state based on the principles of Marx and Lenin. . . . The classical stages as formulated by Marx lent themselves less adequately to the Ethiopian situation than did . . . the actions and political theory of Lenin. . . . In early 1975 . . . the Marxists had gained control of the Dergue, but everything else was still in a state of flux. [Schwab, 1981, pp. 300–1. See K. Marx & F. Engels, 1848; V. Lenin, 1960.]

The forces that moved to take control of the Dergue apparently believed that they had an ideological mission to direct Ethiopia radically to the left. Their decisions and their activities were verification of their task. They steadfastly adhered to their goal, eliminating and opposing all forces who stood in their way. There was an ideological purity and mythical character to this venture that led many in and out of Ethiopia to brand the Dergue as killers. Whatever its image, the Dergue consisted of a group of men who took power, and intended to use it for the benefit of the peasantry of Ethiopia, and were willing to use virtually any means to achieve their ends; to a large extent, the Dergue was often forced into the position of using extreme violence to achieve a successful revolution. As Mengistu maintained in 1978 'the revolution has an obligation to those who have been deprived and oppressed for centuries. Its goal is to build a socialist society in which justice, freedom, equality, and the respect of human rights prevail' (Uwechue, 1978, p. 16). The Dergue became the cutting edge of the revolution.

The soldiers had . . . come a long way from Neghelle barracks revolt. . . . The Dergue no longer saw itself merely as representing the armed forces, but also the millions who had suffered exploitation under the *ancien régime*. . . . Ethiopia's new military rulers were ready to tackle the enormous social problems of Ethiopia. [Ottaway & Ottaway, 1978, p. 62.]

Without question contemporary Africa had never before borne witness to a socialist revolution so overtly based on the ideals and concepts of Marx, Engels and Lenin. The revolution in Ethiopia would be its first, and it was the Dergue that was in the vanguard of the revolution.

Development and Institutionalization of the Revolution

Moving rapidly, the Dergue issued Policy Guidelines on Ethiopian Socialism on 20 December 1974. *Ethiopia Tikdem* (Ethiopian Socialism) was originally explained in the Guidelines which emphasized equality, self-reliance, the dignity of labour and Ethiopian unity. Since Ethiopia traditionally was based on class and status differentials, the concept of equality and dignity of labour struck at the heart of Ethiopian feudalism. '*Ethiopia Tikdem* meant in effect the rejection of a pluralistic parliamentary system in which various interest groups were represented in a struggle to determine national policy. It implied that only some higher body, namely the Dergue, could interpret the common good and steer Ethiopia in the right direction' (ibid., p. 63). The struggle between radicals and liberals within the Dergue had shifted in favour of a socialist direction. *Ethiopia Tikdem* also signified the attack on class stratification, tribal and ethnic differences, and on status being positioned on extracting capital from the abused labour of others within a feudal rubric. The Guidelines suggested that the Dergue place itself in an analogous position to a vanguard party and that governmental institutions and bureaucracy were only to enforce its policy.

In addition, *Ethiopia Tikdem* redefined Ethiopia's economy, calling for a major land reform programme, and reserved the important sectors of the economy for state control, with the private sector being allowed only limited participation. Communications, manufacturing industry, gas, electricity and the exploitation of precious metals and petroleum were to be under state control, while some sectors of surface transportation, food-processing and cottage industry would remain in private hands. Tourism, the paper and pulp industry, large-scale construction, the processing of meats, fruits and vegetables, and mining of metals would be in the hands of the state and private enterprise. This was, in effect, a new economic policy that established the framework upon which a socialist Ethiopia would be constructed. Land reform was the centrepiece of *Ethiopia Tikdem.* The new policy, according to the Guidelines,

> met a long desired need in the peasant population and as such was warmly acclaimed. It also signified that the Dergue was moving away from the concerns of structure towards the process of meeting the economic [and political] needs of its population. The Policy Guidelines on Ethiopian Socialism [was] a major indication that socialism in Ethiopia was to be based on the alteration of property rights moving from a private to a collective system useful for economic progress. [Schwab, 1981, p. 300.]

Although Marxists were in charge within the Dergue and the direction of Ethiopia was now towards socialism, violence between different factions of the left continued until 1978 on the issue of how best to attain a state based on the principles of Marxism–Leninism. New, socialist rules of the political game were established and the framework for political discourse was set by the Dergue. Although the left and right were to continue to mount challenges to the new order, the Dergue after December 1974 was gaining huge support from the peasantry, the class that was to benefit most radically from the proclaimed policies, and in whose name the revolution had been largely fought.

December 1974 was thus a watershed period for Ethiopia. It marked the official introduction of socialist policies, and represented the beginning of the institutionalization of the revolution. From now on the Dergue moved with speed to reaffirm structurally its desire to establish a new social reality for the country. Although it could be argued that *Ethiopia Tikdem* was more in the nature of policy goals than a coherent policy statement, none the less it signified to all Ethiopians that a fairly cohesive framework had been adopted and that all social, political and economic policy that was to follow would be incorporated within that socialist construct. Important, too, was that December 1974 indicated that this would be a revolution from above, a revolution put in place by an elite vanguard of military junior officers. Classical Marxist theory was circumvented and replaced by a policy more in line with Leninism. It was Lenin who formulated the concept of the vanguard party and applied it to Russian society emerging from feudalism. The military Dergue substituted itself for the vanguard party and began to push Ethiopia towards socialism within a Leninist framework. As Mengistu explained in

September 1977, in remarks reflecting the Dergue's directing of the revolution: 'The revolution belongs to the oppressed masses. Therefore, there can be no conflict among us over who was the first to promote the Revolution and be credited by history as such' (*Ethiopian Herald*, 13 September 1977).

During the first two months of 1975 the Dergue nationalized all banks and thirteen insurance companies, and over seventy industrial and commercial companies. In addition the bulk of all manufacturing was placed under the control of the Ministry of Commerce, Industry and Tourism. The first quarter of the new year was politically completed when the land reform programme was announced on 4 March 1975. The Nationalization of Rural Land Proclamation provided for the establishment of peasant associations throughout the country to organize collective farms, distribute land to former tenants and landless persons for personal cultivation, and to handle the economic and social problems inherent in the radical agrarian-reform programme. Each peasant family was granted the free use of a plot of land of less than ten hectares, and the State advocated the establishment of collectives to advance agricultural and economic production. The peasant associations served in a coordinating role, but they also served as a 'form of mass democratic organization' (Berhanu Bayih, 1978, p. 51). According to Berhanu Bayih, of the Standing Committee of PMAC, the peasant associations sent local delegates to district and provincial levels to organize the implementation of land reform. 'They exercise the functions of local self-administration. They have their own executive bodies, judicial bodies, and security agencies. Self-defence detachments have been set up. . . . Their members have been given some military training and provided with weapons' (ibid., pp. 51-2). Such training was considered necessary because of opposition to the land reform programme, particularly by Amhara landlords in the south, and farmers in the north who did not want their traditional land-tenure systems tampered with or disrupted. Until 1977 the peasant associations acted relatively independently of a national government body. In September 1977, in an effort at coordination and centralization, the All-Ethiopian Peasant Association (AEPA) was founded to coordinate the activities of the many peasant associations, which together had organized over seven million farmers.

Landlords, whose land was taken from them could, according to the decree, appeal to a peasant association for compensation, but only for movable property or permanent fixtures, not for the land. To help in the implementation of the nationalization, colleges and secondary schools were shut and students were forced to go into the countryside to aid the peasant associations; this programme was commonly known as *zemecha* (campaign) and was singularly unpopular among the students, whose commitment to the new regime's policies was by no means certain. Many students attempted to organize peasants against the government and as a result many were arrested. The *zemecha* was a notable failure. (See Brietzke, 1976.)

Peasants in the south were elated with the new programme and gave the Dergue wholehearted support. In the north, however, where much of the land was held under ancient communal land-tenure systems, many peasants, particularly in Gojjam province, railed against the proclamation, which they viewed as a destruction of their traditional rights. (Land was held in common by descendants of the original person first granted usage rights and where title remained unfixed. Land, however, was individually farmed.) This opposition was merely a continuation of the political troubles Gojjam caused Haile Selassie in 1967. To the people of Gojjam land, not ideology, was the primary variable. In the north also, the Afar, under the leadership of Sultan Ali Mirreh Hanafare, opposed the new programme. As nomads they were unwilling to accept any fundamental alteration in the usage of their grazing lands. The Afar Liberation Front (ALF) was secretly established and its well-armed population battled with the military and peasant associations when attempts were made to nationalize the land. Individual landlords throughout Ethiopia, but particularly in the south, often refused to accommodate the programme, and they were summarily executed. The Ethiopian Democratic Union (EDU), its membership made up largely of former aristocrats, and based in London and Ethiopia, also opposed the agrarian land reform. It is hardly surprising though that most of the groups that fought vehemently against land reform were often precisely those elements who had benefited under the *ancien régime*.

Overall, the 'land to the tiller' programme was welcomed by the peasant population. Redistributing land in the south to the peasantry, and according them 'possessory rights over the lands they presently till' (Rural Land Proclamation, Art. 19) in the north was a huge success both in terms of land reform, and in tying the peasantry to the Dergue. The Dergue took into limited consideration the concern of communal land farmers in the north by granting them possessory rights.

Between 1975 and 1978, a number of bureaucratic and political problems disallowed effective implementation of the land reform programme. In addition to 60,000 students in the *zemecha* campaign, who in coordination with the EPRP tried to foster opposition to the Dergue and its programme, the Eritreans in the north continued their secessionist war. The increasing battles in the Ogaden against insurgents supported by Somalia, which in 1977 eventually led to a full-scale war, totally disrupted the land reform programme there. Furthermore, urban uprisings against the Dergue forced it to concentrate its policies on opposition in the towns. According to Mengistu 'Counter-revolutionary elements . . . have been conducting a wide range of terror in all parts of the nation' (Uwechue, 1978, p. 16). To shore up and organize the land reform more efficiently, the Dergue in 1978 created the National Revolution Development Campaign and Central Planning Supreme Council which works with the AEPA in order to overcome logistical and political impediments of the programme (see Figure 2). (For additional information on land reform see Brietzke, 1982; Cohen & Koehn, 1977; Hoben, 1975.)

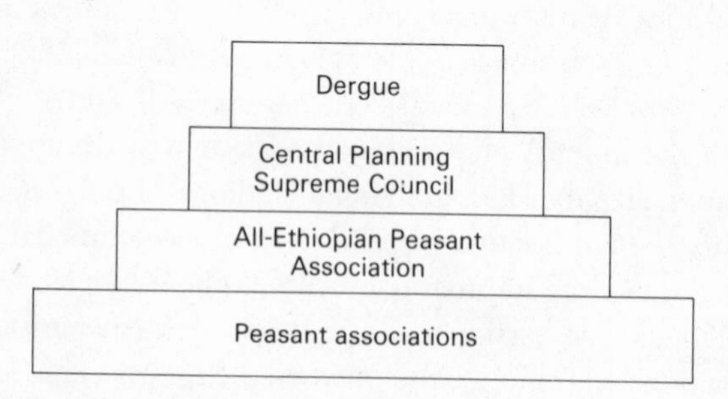

Figure 2. Land Reform: Political Organization

The land reform programme should be evaluated in both economic and political terms. Most Ethiopianists, in opposition to the regime, have concentrated on the former since economically the policy was not very effective. From 1974–8 GDP rose by only 0.4 per cent (*Ten-Year Investment Programme*, 1981), while from 1970–81 its growth rate declined by 50 per cent (World Bank, 1983). From 1973-84 hunger still affected some 15 million people, while by the late 1970s agriculture grew at merely 0.5 per cent, as per capita income at $120 remains the fifth lowest in the world (World Bank, 1980, 1983). Most strikingly, in 1978 food production remained 16 per cent below its level of 1970 (Halliday & Molyneux, 1981). Taking all this into account the Dergue maintained in its *Ten-Year Investment Programme* that it would continue to 'mobilize people's organizations, ... increase the productivity of peasant agriculture, ... and promote peasant production cooperatives'. Even taking into account the political opposition to the land reform policy of the Dergue, the economic performance in the rural areas was disheartening, and remains so. The *Ten-Year Investment Programme*, which is a planning model for the decade 1980-90, implies within its data that much more needs to be done if productivity, particularly in the agricultural sector, is to be increased.

The effectiveness of the Rural Land Proclamation must however also be seen in a political context. It is in this area that land reform and land redistribution has been enormously successful. As a political weapon in the battle for a socialist society land reform struck at the heart of the various opposition movements and securely tied the bulk of the population—the peasantry—to the Dergue and its ideals.

> Land reform became ... the starting point of a concerted campaign to radicalize the peasant masses and to promote the assertion of their class interests. ... The medieval era had come to an end ... and the people of Addis Ababa and other towns staged the largest, most enthusiastic demonstrations the country had ever seen. [Markakis & Ayele, 1978, pp. 132-3.]

The political importance of land reform far outweighs the present economic ineffectiveness, because, in effect, land reform produced the support for the new government that was vital if the Dergue and its Marxist representatives were to survive the violence and opposition in the period 1975-8. In addition the proclamation gave legitimacy to the Dergue and its political platform. It also integrated the peasants into the revolution. As Mao Tse-tung stated 'If you want to know the taste of a pear you must change the pear by eating it yourself. ... If you want to know the theory and methods of revolution, you must participate in revolution' (Mao Tse-tung, 1962, p. 205). After centuries of oppression, the peasants were able not only to participate in a revolution but to experience its benefits; and from this, vast political support was generated from the peasantry to the Dergue. There is every prospect that at some future time economic benefits will flow from the land reform programme. In my view, without the political aspect the economic changes would be less than meaningful. By first advocating and then installing a radical nationalization and redistribution land policy, the Dergue effected the most necessary and cleverest programme. Henceforth, the Dergue would be able to count on the political and psychological support of the peasants, and the student and provincial opposition would find itself in a political vacuum. The Dergue became the articulator of peasant interests and no other group, no matter what its political ideology, would reasonably be able to speak for the peasants. The shrill cry that eventually came from the students and the EPRP that the Dergue was not radical enough and was motivated by personal, political and ideological self-interest would fall on deaf ears in the countryside. The Dergue, by its implementation of the most radical of land reform programmes, had locked-in the support of the peasantry. It seems very clear that this decision was of fundamental political importance and was the key factor in the Dergue's success against all its internal opponents. Whether all this was known in advance of the decision itself is very doubtful; but the decision, motivated by a desire to do something, finally, for the peasants, and to secure the leftist ideology of the Dergue, none the less was vital to the battle against domestic enemies.

The establishment of the peasant associations and its attendant bureaucracy created something of a petty bourgeoisie in the countryside, since individuals were recruited from the cities to assist the peasant associations. At the same time because of the miserable state of education in Ethiopia at this time and earlier (see, *School Census for Ethiopia*, 1967-73), few well-trained individuals existed to fill the roles in the bureaucracy. This was made even more acute by the opposition of so many students who were initially called by the Dergue to go into the country to assist in the land reform's implementation. Thus, the political success of land reform *vis-à-vis* the peasants is even more startling.

The establishment and implementation of the land reform programme was a significant period in the history of revolutionary and socialist Ethiopia. It defined the Dergue's support of the needs of the peasants, and it allowed the peasants to experience the results of the revolution, thus eliciting their support. It froze opposition groups out of the real political arena because it disallowed them from seeking major support from the peasants. It clarified the direction that Ethiopia would follow and it signalled the Dergue's determination to control the political process. The radical nature of the new government was now in the open for all to see, and whether the names of the Dergue members were known or not, its policy was becoming clearer—the social system was moving sharply to the left and the Dergue was in control. By 1981 more than eleven million peasants had come under the authority of the AEPA, and as a result of the National Revolution Development Campaign agricultural output rose almost 5 per cent. The Dergue then began to consider expanding the number of collectives which was a natural outflow from its 1978 decision to restrict individual plot usage to far less then ten hectares. Some opposition to this expansion was registered in the southern provinces, particularly Sidamo, and resulted in a slowing down of the collectivization programme. Nevertheless, by 1984 there was every indication that land reform was here to stay and its expansion into more radical forms might, at some point, be implemented.

The third major period defining the development of the revolution and the Dergue (following *Ethiopia Tikdem*, and land reform) was represented by the 26 July 1975 Government Ownership of Urban Lands and Extra Houses Proclamation. The decree nationalized urban land, and allowed urban inhabitants to become members of a cooperative or urban dwellers' association, the 'kebelle'. Each urban area was divided into sections administered by a kebelle overseeing between 200 and 500 households (Cohen & Koehn, 1977, p. 31). In Addis Ababa alone, 294 associations were established. Each kebelle had the power to make political and administrative decisions in its neighbourhood and to see to it that these decisions were carried out. In order to do that, each comprised a judicial body composed of three members empowered to enforce its regulations. According to Article 30 of the Proclamation, 'no person who has exhausted his right of appeal at the kebelle judicial tribunals may lodge an appeal to the ordinary courts of law'. According to Norman J. Singer, 'the creation of the kebelle courts was presumably an attempt to introduce into the urban areas a set of courts that would be more responsive to the needs of the ordinary people' (1978, p. 23). Disputes over housing allotments and urban land are the most typical of the cases heard. Individuals are appointed to a kebelle by the Dergue or elected by the community. The kebelles, in their power and structure, are similar to the *barios* in Angola, and to some degree to *Poder Popular* in Cuba.

Proclamation 104 of October 1976 clarified and made explicit the powers and duties of the kebelles. Accordingly, kebelles were charged with municipal administration, housing redistribution, establishing cooperative retail food outlets, renting houses, encouraging voluntary associations, particularly women's organizations, and creating self-help projects. They were also empowered to build roads, register all social arrangements such as births and weddings, establish postal, educational, health and recreational facilities, and to develop literacy programmes.

Like the peasant associations, the kebelles were established by the Dergue in an effort to decentralize the structures of authority and incorporate the urban proletariat and petty bourgeoisie into the revolution. Although there was rapid centralization, in structural form, of the peasant associations for the sake of their effectiveness, the Dergue has left the kebelles in place. However, since in practice most kebelle officials are appointed by the Dergue, the kebelles often act as the urban arm of the Dergue, promoting its policies and implementing its decisions.

Still, the creation of the kebelles was a revolutionary act. In Ethiopia multiple numbers of urban homes were owned by a single landlord. Nationalization of urban houses left only one house per person, with the kebelles empowered to ensure equitable distribution. Although it must be said that landlords sometimes circumvented the decree by redistributing houses to their family members. The kebelles drew the urban population directly into revolutionary activity and serve as a local, political-judicial organization that gives urban inhabitants a perception of greater authority. In some cases kebelles have acted so independently that the Dergue has had to limit their power. 'Girma Kebede was executed in April 1977, accused of murdering 24 people and torturing many others while chairman of the Arat Kilo Kebelle in Addis Ababa' (Brietzke, 1982, p. 296; see also Amnesty International, 1977).

The Dergue armed the kebelles in 1976 and called for them to go on the offensive and administer 'revolutionary justice' to counter-revolutionaries. Subsequently, summary execution then took place and undermined the original purpose of the kebelles. 'It was no longer necessary to bring a dispute to the tribunal as long as there were other forces like the kebelle guards who were willing to administer justice summarily' (Singer, op. cit., p. 24). As a result of Mengistu's directive, from 1976 to 1978, kebelles far exceeded their legal authority by abusing their power over those inhabitants under their control. For three years popular support for the kebelles turned to fear. Although the Dergue curtailed this activity of the kebelles after 1978, it will take some time for the kebelles to once again obtain full popular support.

Theoretically, the kebelle concept was a radical innovation. It incorporated the urban poor and the middle class into the revolution; the benefits were distributed to the urban poor while the middle and upper classes had to abide by the dictates of equality. By 1980 more than 3,000 kebelles had been established in the cities and towns of Ethiopia with millions of people participating in their activity in one way or another. The kebelles and the peasant associations together 'develop the political education of the masses, the reconstruction of public life [and] educating the masses . . . on Marxist-Leninist propaganda' (*Pravda*, 19 June 1981). At the same time the kebelle, along with the peasant association, gave to the peasant and working class a degree of power and authority that they had never imagined would be theirs. Though the Dergue was the most powerful institution in the country, it could not do everything, and kebelles and peasant associations were given a substantial amount of authority. While peasant associations eventually lost a large proportion of their authority, the kebelles retained much of theirs. Both structures were successful attempts to spread the revolution to the masses with the Dergue acting out its role directing the revolution from the top. To paraphrase Che Guevara's discussion of the Cuban revolution, the Ethiopian revolution along with peasant associations and kebelles were both tank and tractor, the one 'breaking down in its passage the barriers . . . and [the other] creating new social relationships' (Guevara in Mazlish, *et al.*, 1971, p. 404).

On 20 April 1976, the Dergue launched a campaign that was to further consolidate the revolution. The Ethiopian National Democratic Revolution Programme (ENDRP) was designed to fuse together the gains of the revolution and to establish future norms. The primary goals of ENDRP as announced by Mengistu were the

> elimination of feudalism, bureaucratic capitalism and imperialism . . . to build a new people's Ethiopia. . . . To this end, a People's Democratic Republic will be established . . . under the leadership of the proletariat in close collaboration with the farmers, the

support of the petty bourgeois, anti-feudalist and anti-imperialist forces to guarantee to the Ethiopian people their right to freedom, equality, unity, peace and prosperity. [*The Ethiopian Herald*, 21 April 1976.]

It also proclaimed that the Dergue would 'lay a firm foundation for a transition to socialism [and that] the historical rights . . . of every nationality would be given equal respect' (ibid.). A one-party revolutionary state based on socialism was the ultimate goal. A fifteen-member Political Bureau or Provisional Office for Mass Organizational Affairs (POMOA), under the leadership of Haile Fida, a French-educated Marxist, was created to advise the Dergue on the implementation of the ENDRP. According to Berhanu Bayih, the ENDRP is the basic Ethiopian document laying down guidelines for the revolutionary process:

It establishes Ethiopia's entry upon the path of socialist orientation and sets as the goal of the national democratic stage the formation of a people's democratic republic led by the working class party. When we call our country 'Socialist Ethiopia' we do not mean that we have already built up a socialist society. We are now at the stage of national democratic revolution. And we are aware that it will take much time before we can go over to socialist construction. [Bayih, 1978, p. 51.]

The ENDRP must be analysed in the light of established objectives, rather than from the perspective of present-day events. The programme was certainly the most formative exposition of the goals of socialist Ethiopia. It took into consideration both structure and process and recognized the contradictions that had to be dealt with. In admitting the existence of ethnic rebellions and maintaining that it would recognize the rights of nationalities, the Dergue indicated it would attempt to deal with the issue of ethnic minorities. In September 1976, Teferi Banti, chairman of the Dergue, went even further and said that the Dergue would accept regional autonomy for Ethiopia's various nationalities (*New York Times*, 13 September 1976). Although the goal of socialism is theoretically the obliteration of national distinctions, the nationalities question in Ethiopia is so complex that recognition of its importance was taken into account. In essence the ENDRP clarified the revolutionary goals of Ethiopia, and called for a party structure through which these goals could be attained.

The ENDRP was launched within a historical perspective and was thus rooted in the revolutionary process, which itself laid the framework for the attainment of ENDRP's goals:

In the short span of time since February 1974, the revolutionary movement of the Ethiopian people has attained several major victories. On the economic front, all rural land has been nationalized; urban land and extra houses have been put under government control; banks, industries, and insurance companies have become public property. . . . These measures have shaken the feudo-capitalist system at its base. On the political front, the major victory is . . . the removal of the emperor . . ., the dealing of death blows to feudal lackeys and thereby the heralding of the complete abolition of the archaic autocratic monarchical rule which has remained the mainstay of feudal Ethiopia. This has also resulted in the awakening of the masses. Socialism has also been declared as the guiding principle of the revolution. And this has opened the way for the public propagation of the socialist world outlook.

In order to consolidate and give these victories a lasting premise and increase popular participation in the overall revolutionary process, it is imperative that the broad masses be politicized, organized and armed. The [Dergue], on various occasions, has declared its clear intention to transfer state power to the broad masses. Therefore, in order to enable all anti-feudal and anti-imperialist forces to organize freely, and in order to establish a united front under the leadership of the working class party which can establish a people's democratic state [ENDRP] has been issued. Uniting and leading the broad masses through the national democratic revolution is the only road to . . . socialism. [Ethiopian National Democratic Revolution Programme, 20 April 1976.]

As one interested observer stated: the ENDRP is part of the social revolution that 'is bringing the masses of workers and peasants into intense struggle and organization on behalf of their class interests' (Griswold, 1978a, p. 1).

ENDRP was a far more sophisticated blueprint for Ethiopia's future than the 1974 policy guidelines of *Ethiopia Tikdem*. For not only did it spell out in more detail the parameters of socialist ideology, but it dealt with evident contradictions which needed resolution. It created a new political institution, the POMOA, comprising civilian Marxists who were called upon to advise the Dergue. Presumably, the Dergue was trying to incorporate civilian intellectuals into the system thereby broadening its political base. The ENDRP played an important role in defining the direction the Dergue would take and clarified more precisely its socialist bent. This was an important theoretical milestone in the post-revolutionary history of Ethiopia; it virtually sanctified the new socialist culture and orientation that was now part of Ethiopia.

Almost from the very first days of its takeover of the government apparatus, the Dergue was confronted by enemies on both the left and right, and from the centre. The manner in which the Dergue eventually came to oppose those forces was, in this author's opinion, the primary defining characteristic of the Ethiopian revolution and was thus a clear demarcation point in the development of the regime. This fifth major period defining the development of the Dergue was unequivocal in its clarity and starkly defined the lengths the Dergue was willing to go to ensure the success of the revolution. The tactics and the violence used to defend and expand the revolution were contradictory in that they broadened the list of opponents while at the same time flushing them out and eliminating them as political actors. The final result of its violent actions was the total defeat of its enemies, the strengthening of the Dergue's political role, and the legitimation of the revolution, allowing the Dergue to concentrate on policies that could improve the economic position of all Ethiopians.

When the Dergue first took power, decisions were as far as possible made on a democratic basis. But as the Marxists gained power within the Dergue, those that were seen by Mengistu Haile Mariam as opposing his brand of Marxism were labelled counter-revolutionaries. 'By 1975 democratic decision-making was being rapidly undermined as power moved to the hard core of Marxists within the Dergue. Mengistu, the real power behind the Dergue, firmly believed in imposing Marxism from above using any amount of violence necessary for the successful achievement of a socialist state' (Schwab, 1981, p. 303). As he said in 1978

> Our struggle is a calculated and scientific attempt to neutralize the power of the reactionary forces which are trying to destroy our revolution at its very birth. Those who have been dispossessed have reacted . . . and are being successfully fought by the broad masses. [Uwechue, 1978, p. 16.]

> Mengistu, like Lenin, was willing to force the population to accept socialism, believed in a leadership cadre, and was absolutely unwilling to await the democratic revolution that would evolve from a protracted people's struggle. Mengistu thus moved to consolidate his power, and to eliminate his enemies within the Dergue and PMAC who were more [or less] 'purist' than he. [Schwab, op. cit., pp. 303–4.]

In 1974, then, the 'second Ethiopian revolution' began, a revolution that would establish Mengistu as the leader of the Dergue, and the Dergue the vanguard of the revolution.

After November 1974 when sixty Ethiopian notables and aristocrats were executed Mengistu moved against his opponents on the left. From July 1975 to September 1976, over a hundred members of the Dergue and military officials who worked along with it were executed, including

Major Sisay Habte, the Third Vice-chairman of PMAC. By early 1977 it was reported that 'perhaps as few as twenty' of the original members of the Dergue had survived the purges (Legum & Lee, 1977, pp. 18, 42). The power struggle within the Dergue reached its climax on 3 February 1977, when at a meeting of the Dergue seven of its leading members were shot and killed by Mengistu and his supporters. Among the dead were the PMAC Chairman Teferi Banti, and Captains Alemayehu Haile and Mogus Wolde-Michael, all of whom in December 1976 had attempted to restrict the power of Mengistu and Atnafu Abate. Mengistu became Chairman of the PMAC, Head of State, and Commander-in-Chief of the armed forces. Atnafu was put in charge of the people's militia, which in the rural areas was responsible for preserving order. Mengistu began at once to centralize his authority by eliminating all his opponents (or perceived opponents) within the Dergue and by combining the Dergue and the PMAC. Almost all power within the Dergue was in Mengistu's hands. He acquired complete control of the regime in November 1977 when Atnafu Abate was executed. Now only Berhanu Bayih and Mengistu remained of the original group of top military officers in the Dergue.

On 4 February, one day after the Dergue shoot-out, Mengistu made plain his future intentions. At a mass rally he maintained that

> As a result of the determined and decisive step taken [yesterday] . . . against the internal collaborators and supporters of the EPRP, EDU, ELF, our Revolution has . . . advanced from the defensive to the offensive. . . . Henceforth we will tackle enemies that come face to face with us and we will not be stabbed from behind by internal foes. . . . To this end, we will arm the allies and comrades of the broad masses without giving respite to reactionaries and avenge the blood of our comrades double and triplefold. [*Ethiopian Herald*, 5 February 1977.]

After November 1977, Mengistu, in an attempt to consolidate his political power further in the face of multiple opposition, altered the existing Dergue structure. The Dergue would continue to exist, but decisions would be made by a Standing Committee of sixteen members. A Central Committee of thirty-two representatives would make recommendations to the Standing Committee. The General Congress of the Dergue included all forty-eight members. Mengistu remained Chairman of the Dergue (now synonymous with the PMAC) and continued as Head of State. Despite the structure of the Dergue, Mengistu eclipsed all its other members, made most decisions himself, and 'assumed increasingly more of the trappings of power' (Legum & Lee, 1977, p. 89). Previously five Marxist-Leninist parties acceptable to the Dergue were permitted to articulate their political views: the All-Ethiopian Socialist Movement (*Me'ison*), the Marxist-Leninist Revolutionary Organization, the Revolutionary Seded, the Labour League, and the Revolutionary Struggle of the Oppressed Peoples of Ethiopia. Despite their existence, their ability to influence the Dergue was limited. In June 1977 the five groups were merged into the United Front of Ethiopian Marxist-Leninist Organizations. The authority wielded by the United Front was no greater than its predecessors (see Figure 3). In December 1979, however, an entirely new umbrella organization was created to organize a vanguard political party that was to be established at some future time.

There is no person who is more of a true believer in the current revolution than Mengistu. The son of an Amhara soldier and a Shankella mother, he once maintained that his enemies 'may succeed in assassinating me or other revolutionaries, but . . . regardless of who dies, our Revolution will continue' (*Granma*, 7 May 1978). A ruthless advocate of his Marxist political philosophy, he appears willing to eliminate any person or group who opposes his beliefs. This was seen in his revolt against the Dergue; and it would be seen again in his war against the forces of opposition outside the Dergue. Together the two battles entailed the 'second Ethiopian revolution'.

The EPRP's offensive against the Dergue took on bloody and serious overtones in 1976 when it began a campaign of terror that included assassination of labour union, kebelle and Dergue officials. Made up of urban intellectuals, college and secondary students, the EPRP maintained that a Marxist revolution cannot be directed through a military machine, and argued that class contradictions can only be provoked through a period of multi-party democracy, during which time a people's revolution will take place (see Markakis & Ayele, 1978; Ottaway & Ottaway, 1978; Halliday & Molyneux, 1981). It defined the policy of the Dergue as 'adventurism' and claimed to adhere to the theories of Mao Tse-tung, whose revolution in China was based on wide-ranging peasant participation.

By 1976 the Dergue had laid the foundations of the new state, both in theory and practice. Through *Ethiopia Tikdem*, ENDRP, the land reform programme, and the urban land edict, the Dergue had garnered the support of a huge majority of its population and had begun to legitimize

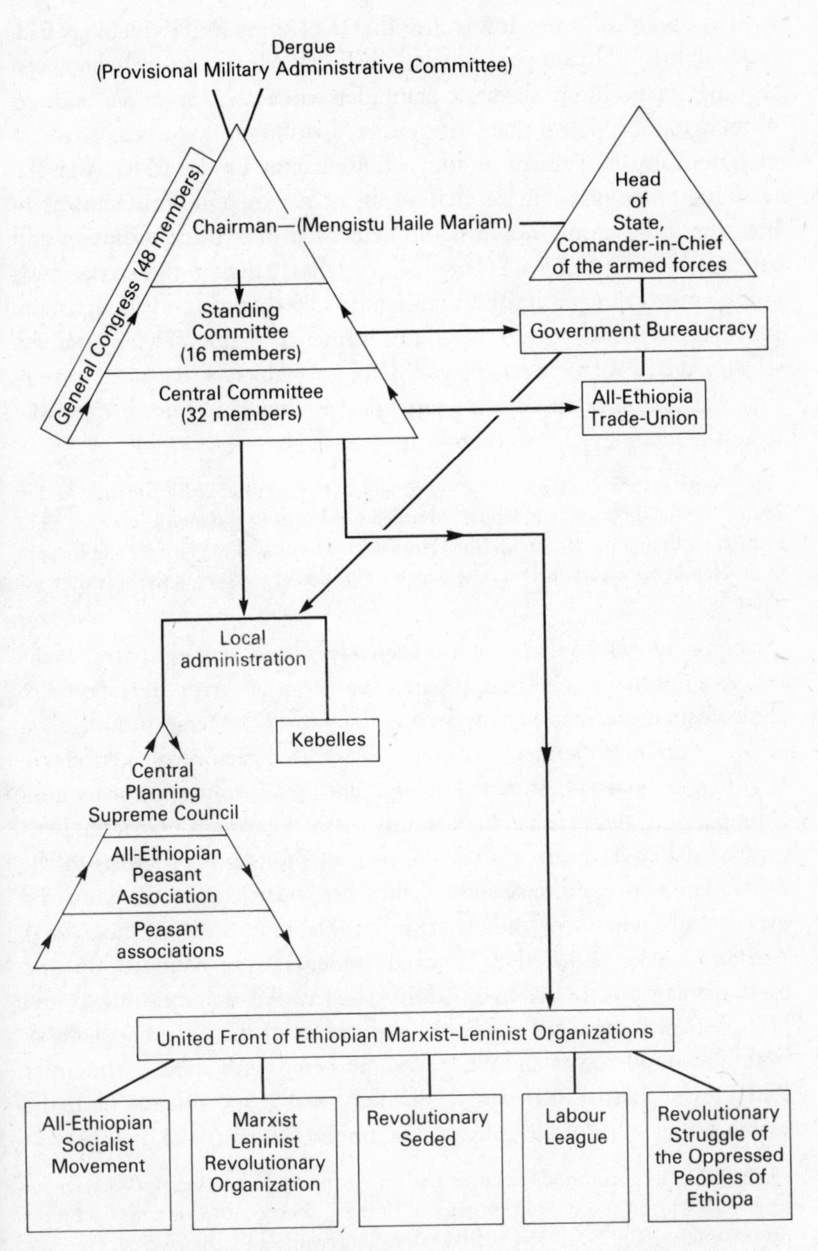

Figure 3. Socialist Ethiopia (1977): The Political Structure

itself as a political entity. It was clear that the Dergue and its ideology had, in attracting public support, isolated the EPRP, which until 1976 had been arguing its positions through pamphlets such as *Democracia*, and via mimeographed sheets that were either distributed on streetcorners or plastered on the walls of buildings. Discussions by the EPRP over the meaning of its programme, definitions of words, and arguments as to how the programme should be implemented took place in homes and cafes. While the EPRP was busy over-intellectualizing, the Dergue was engaged in running a revolution. Engulfed by rhetoric and thought, the EPRP had virtually given away any influence it might have attained. Clearly, the EPRP membership could not grasp the fact that a real revolution was taking place; to some large degree they could not break away from the ideology of the classroom.

> What looks surprising is why [anyone] should have given the EPRP the time of day. They were for the most part foreign educated Leftists from the middle class. . . .They insisted on having no truck with [the Dergue]. . . .They failed to grasp the significance of developments within their society which had found expression in the armed forces. [Gott, 1982.]

Recognizing in 1976 that they had been left behind, representatives of the EPRP, acting from weakness, began a campaign of terror. In response to the assassinations that were occurring daily in 1977 Mengistu unleashed what he called a campaign of 'red terror': 'Red terror will henceforth engulf the quarters of reaction and counter-revolution throughout Ethiopia' (*Ethiopian Herald*, 18 November 1977). Through 1978 it has been estimated that 'red terror' took the lives of thousands of leftists of the EPRP. The police, military and kebelles were instructed to flush out and execute all enemies of the government (Halliday & Molyneux, 1981). Earlier, in May 1977, five hundred students were rounded up and executed. For a year citizens of Addis Ababa awoke each morning to find bodies strewn along the sidewalks and streets of the city. The walls of buildings in all towns and cities were plastered with signs to 'Intensify Red Terror'. The EPRP was decimated, unable to contend with the violence that it had itself unleashed (Amnesty International, 1978).

> The EPRP, by its purism and resentment, failed to support the new socialist government precisely at the historical moment that was of the greatest consequence for the Ethiopian peasantry. The EPRP had misjudged the moment, and in its own peculiar way placed itself in a counter-revolutionary role. It was in the contradictory position of

calling itself socialist and opposing the institution of socialism in Ethiopia. [Schwab, 1982, p. 192.]

Or, to put it a bit differently, 'The EPRP . . . characterizes the Dergue as "fascist", a term that does not indicate that they have yet comprehended the nature of the state in contemporary Ethiopia . . . , no fascist regime ever carried out a land reform' (Halliday & Molyneux, op. cit., p. 125). The left in Ethiopia, as represented by the EPRP, had miscalculated and could not deal with a real revolution. It was enmeshed in confusion, contradiction and resentment at being excluded by the Dergue. (For an analysis of the left in Ethiopia see Schwab, 1982.) Spending its early years involved in intellectual discourse that turned out to be irrelevant, it turned to violence when it saw the developing legitimacy of the Dergue. But in its usual unrealistic and academic style it failed to foresee that the Dergue would react with greater and more efficient violence. By 1978 the EPRP was finished as a political force with most of its membership either dead, in jail, or in exile.

Until 1977, the Confederation of Ethiopian Labour Unions (CELU) also opposed the policies of the Dergue, maintaining that revolution had to come from below, and should not be imposed from above. In response, the Dergue had arrested or executed most of its leadership, and in January 1977 it replaced the CELU with the All-Ethiopia Trade Union (AETU). (For a discussion of CELU see below and see Ottaway, 1976.) Also in 1977, the Dergue announced the arrest of Haile Fida of POMOA who was charged with using *Me'ison* and POMOA to take power by seeking control of the kebelles, the government ministries, and the trade union using the Yekatit 66 ideological school as his vanguard (Bayih, 1978). He was apparently executed some time later.

The tragedy and irony of the opposition stemming from EPRP and CELU is that both groups were advocating what the Dergue was implementing. Although they insisted that their dispute with the Dergue was purely ideological it appears evident that personalism played a large role in their confrontations with the Dergue. 'Excluded from power despite their role in helping to lead and organize the revolution [they] felt betrayed that the military had taken all positions of power' (Schwab, 1982, p. 191). The EPRP, particularly, acted like spoiled academics and almost asked to be crushed by the revolution. In not understanding that a *real* revolution was taking place and was transforming Ethiopia along the ideological lines they ought truly to have supported, the EPRP missed the boat. What was occurring in Ethiopia was neither game-theory nor an academic exercise; yet the EPRP acted as if it were. In so doing the EPRP was in fact counter-revolutionary and forced the Dergue into the violent position that it took. That violence clarified the determination of the Dergue and marked an important stage in the development of the revolution.

So 1977 was an important and extraordinary year for the Ethiopian revolution. It marked the emergence of Mengistu as the leading figure of the Dergue, and clarified the extent to which Mengistu would go to further the revolution. In dismantling the liberal CELU he eliminated the only available political structure in which the centre could find a home. This was all accomplished through the politics of violence and execution. To a very large degree Mengistu was following the theoretical framework established by Frantz Fanon (1968). Incorporating violence as a cleansing force Mengistu was, after 1977, free to pursue his goals and move to establish socialism in Ethiopia. The year 1977 was one in which all personal, political and ideological disputes were settled; and their resolution came out of the barrel of the gun. After 1977 no opposition to the new order would be tolerated, and violence became a major weapon of the revolution. This was not the socialism of Allende's Chile or of Nicaragua, both of which were tolerant of opposition groups. The Ethiopian revolution was to be far more radical and far less tolerant. It is almost certain that within this violence personal disputes were settled, and clearly this ought not to be condoned. On the other hand, those who maintain that the Ethiopian revolution is far too violent and thus must be condemned have missed the point. It was not the Dergue that initiated the violence against the civilian opposition. Mengistu and the Dergue made it clear that they would use violence to the deadliest extent necessary to maintain the revolution. Confronted by opposition in the cities, within the Dergue, in Eritrea, in the Ogaden, in Tigre and from Somalia, Mengistu decided that if he did not eliminate those he considered counter-revolutionary, they would eliminate him and prevent socialism from being instituted in Ethiopia.

Thus by 1977, the parameters of the Ethiopian revolution were clear. A political structure was in place, a theoretical base had been established (see Figure 4), socialist concepts were institutionalized in the cities and in the interior, and a punishing violence had been established as the norm of enforcement. The preconditions for the establishment of a socialist Ethiopia were now in place. The ensuing years would see a further development and legitimization of socialist values: 1974–7 was the formative period of Ethiopian socialism—a new political tradition was in the early stages of being established—its advancement would be seen in the years 1978–83.

More than anything else however, 1977 resolved the class warfare that prevented effective application of the revolution through the country, for it was the bourgeois and middle-class 'revolutionaries' that were destroyed. Many of the students who were members of the EPRP were

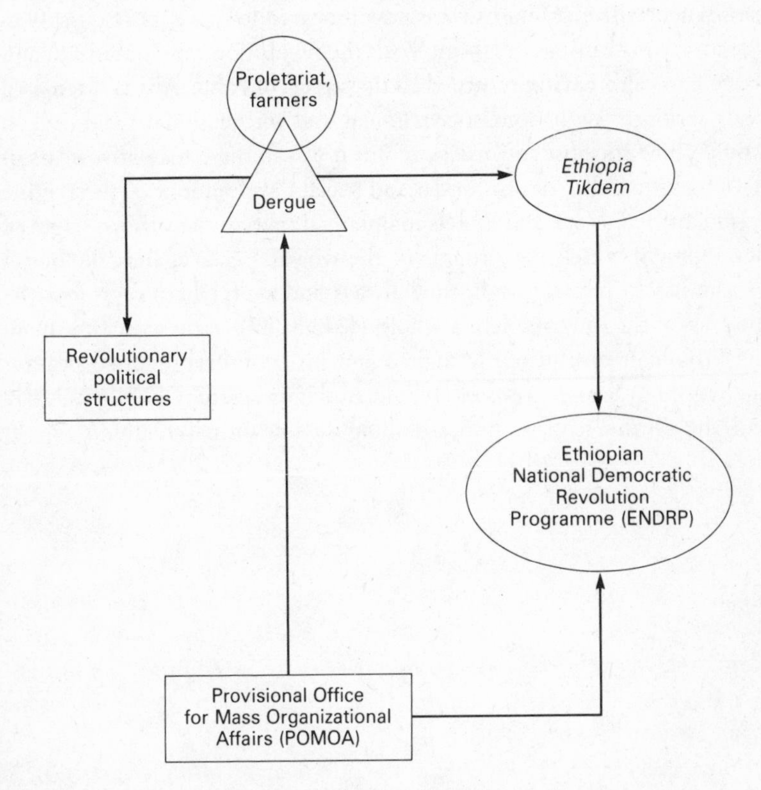

Figure 4. Socialist Ethiopia (1977): The Theoretical Base

sons and daughters of those who held positions of dominance prior to the revolution. It was this group who through *zemecha* and via their leaflets tried to disrupt the direction of socialism. Those truly representing the peasant and working class came out on top in this class confrontation that rumbled through Ethiopia like an earthquake. The tumultuous class battles that raged on the streets, in the countryside and inside officialdom, defined the political and ideological characteristics of the victors. The struggle served to clarify Mengistu's position that the conservative and bourgeois element that once so oppressed Ethiopia would be destroyed; the violence of the executions served as a cleansing agent. As Fanon so well put it, the destruction 'is the preliminary to the unification of the people' (Fanon, 1968, p. 94).

With theory and policy in place, and with the middle and upper classes neutralized, Mengistu was now prepared to move more quickly in effectively instituting socialism. With the revolution now stabilized, and peace and calm having returned to the streets of Addis Ababa, Mengistu dealt seriously with domestic, regional and international issues which would allow socialist construction. But it was in these formative years of the revolution that the historical and social development of the regime was identified. Marx and Engels maintained that 'in the various stages of development which the struggle of the working class against the bourgeoisie has to pass through, they always and everywhere represent the interests of the movement as a whole' (1848, p. 23). In these early years in the Ethiopian revolution, Mengistu and his group represented peasant and working-class interests as a whole. And it was certain that they clearly had 'the advantage of . . . understanding the line of march' (ibid.).

2 The Political System

The Centre

By virtually implementing Stalin's 1927 edict of 'class vs. class' Mengistu and his allies within the Dergue were now able to turn their attention to the further development and formation of socialism, and to regional and foreign policy (see Chapter 4). Although the Dergue had made clear its socialist direction, the institutionalization of socialism would require the development of a political system in which civilians participated in the political process through the rubric of a vanguard structure. This was also the direction that the USSR desired to see in Ethiopia and it 'encouraged the drive for a political party' (Halliday & Molyneux, 1981, p. 142). After 1977 military/civilian relations improved markedly and the Dergue concentrated on establishing a vanguard political entity.

In the early years of the revolution the struggle between the Dergue radicals and the opposing civilian forces laid bare the fact that the military junior officers were the true vanguard of the revolution. It was they who pressured for the revolution, and who kept it going despite all obstacles. And it was this group that created a revolution from above, and then integrated those forces from below who represented the classes, and who were the classes for which the revolution was being fought. It was the Dergue that toppled the old government and insisted on developing a new socialist system. Through the struggle the patterns of class were more clearly defined, but the outcome of the early period of class struggle required that the issue of class formation now be dealt with. It is within this framework that the USSR and forces within Ethiopia pressured for the implementation of Lenin's dictum that 'only a party that will organize really nation-wide exposures can become the vanguard of the revolutionary forces' (Lenin, in Mazlish, 1971, p. 160). Inside Ethiopia and particularly within the Dergue there was not a universal consensus that the military should lay aside their uniforms; but it was concurrently recognized that Lenin's policy was an accurate formation of socialist historical necessity. Neither the original theoreticians of Marxism, nor the primary interpreters of it ever accepted a military junta as playing a vanguard role in the revolution. Because this was the case in Ethiopia it was both an original situation and a contradiction. The military *was* the vanguard in Ethiopia and thus it added an innovative dimension to the history of socialism. However, because it was also a contradiction the Dergue, in part through Soviet pressure, and in some part through its own theoretical perspective, moved to resolve the contradiction in the years 1978 and 1979. Its resolution was also original since it created a vanguard political structure that both incorporated the Dergue and yet allowed the Dergue to hold an independent political existence outside the new structure.

One can therefore look at the Dergue's role in the Ethiopian revolution as a newly evolved model for socialist change: it represented the revolutionary forces in the country and in organizing and leading the continuing revolution.

It marked the first time in Africa, and indeed in the Third World, that such a revolution had been sparked and emplaced by a military spearhead that had its roots in the old regime. This revolution and the political system it created was unlike any that have been related to the Ethiopian struggle. The Free Officers Movement in Egypt was hardly Marxist; the struggle in Angola, Mozambique and Guinea-Bissau was primarily an anti-imperialist struggle led by indigenous guerrillas; the Cuban revolution was organized by insurgents who were neither soldiers nor part of any existing governmental structure; and the Afghanistan war is a civil war that the Soviet Union has seen fit to involve itself in directly. Chile under Allende and Sandinista Nicaragua were both in the nature of social reform movements with a very limited trace of true radicalism, while the case of Zimbabwe points to a New Deal type of Marxism that only recently has moved toward violence. Both Benin and the People's Republic of the Congo are examples of socialism via the coup, neither incorporating the radical anti-feudal and anti-traditional nature of the Dergue. And the lengthy anti-colonial struggle in Indo-China led by Ho Chi Minh, a political example in and of itself, was totally unlike the Ethiopian revolution. Ethiopia, then, stands alone and its revolution is a radical historical departure from contemporary and previous socialist movements in the Third World. With the establishment of the Commission to Organize the Party of the Working People of Ethiopia (COPWE) the Dergue maintained its originality but moved ever closer to traditional and orthodox socialism.

The creation in 1979 of COPWE reinforced Ethiopia's position as a new socialist role model as this political structure (1) was also created from above by the Dergue, (2) integrated the Dergue while also permitting it its own autonomous existence, (3) reflected the Dergue's perception that militarism would now move to a politicization of the revolution, and (4) recognized that COPWE would aid the process of class formation that would then permit at some future time the establishment of an orthodox vanguard party. Mengistu developed the latter point in 1981: 'Though not a party, [COPWE] is currently playing the role of a workers' party. Thus the formation of tomorrow's workers' party is inseparably linked with today's COPWE' (Addis Ababa Domestic Service, 1 May 1981). It was further clarified by Legesse Asfaw, of COPWE and the Dergue, when he stated that COPWE is part of 'a strategy for action [to] speed up the development of the incipient [communist] party which will soon emerge' (*Granma*, 4 June 1981).

Through 1978 and 1979 discussions as to what form the new political entity should take went on within the Dergue, between the Dergue and civilian representatives, and between Mengistu and the Soviet Union. In the latter part of 1979 the Dergue announced that POMOA and all political groups within the United Front of Ethiopian Marxist-Leninist Organizations were to be dissolved; in December it announced the creation of COPWE, stressing that membership was available on an individual, rather than on a group basis. After 1979 then, the political structure was revised and the Ethiopian revolution moved to a new, more formative stage of its development (see Figure 5). The Dergue had taken a rather large step in organizing COPWE. It relegated to the past the violence that drove it to the top of the political order and appeared intent on moving into more traditional spheres of activity. The civilian opposition had been stilled and the Dergue could now afford to work together with civilians who supported its policies without fearing that the opposing forces would gain the upper hand. Other than enemies in Eritrea and the Ogaden that the Dergue would contend with, the opposition had been muted. Order was now in the process of being restored, and it was COPWE that symbolized the new, more political and traditional order and the legitimation of the revolution within doctrinaire political norms.

In 1980 two Ethiopianists stated that 'given the absence of a mass-based

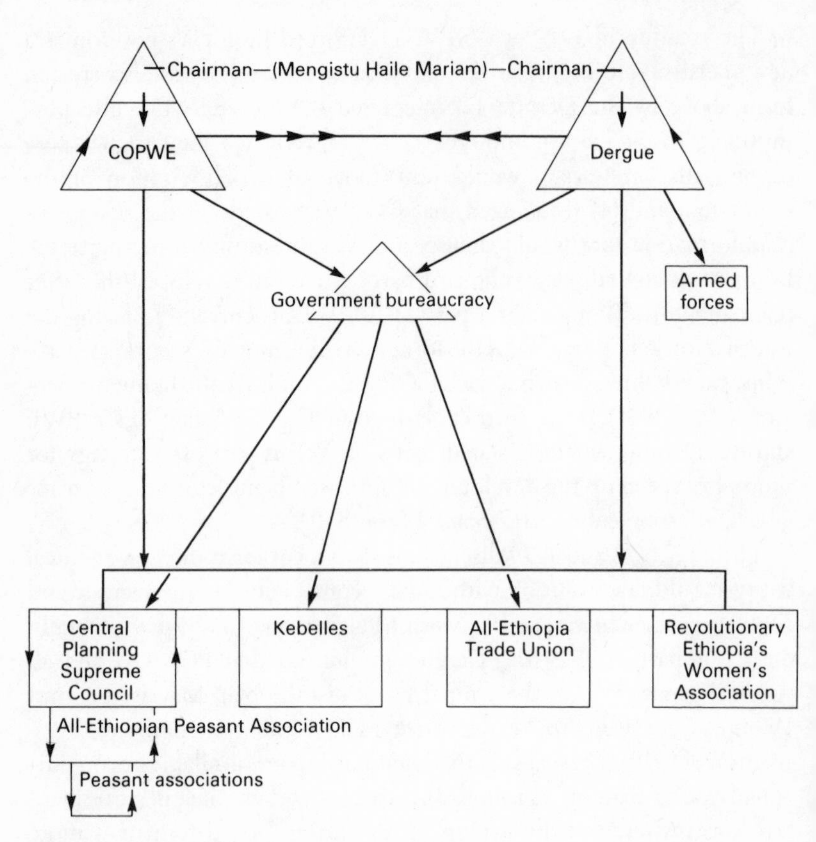

Figure 5. Socialist Ethiopia: The Political System

political party with a coherent and unifying ideology . . . it is difficult to envision how . . . Ethiopia could be expected to move other than in a loosely integrated and exceedingly variable direction' (Cohen & Koehn, 1980, p. 302). The creation of COPWE with the ideological base of *Ethiopia Tikdem* and ENDRP represented the Dergue's attempt to confront this issue. Although the hierarchy of COPWE and the Dergue are virtually identical, the movement towards a central political organization indicated a policy shift away from a military value orientation and towards a political one. The military aspects of the revolution were giving way, though slowly to be sure, and the population as a whole was being integrated into a highly-centralized pre-party mechanism. Now that civil peace had been restored, the Dergue clarified through the establishment of COPWE that it would continue its rapid and radical shift to the left but it would now do so via a political route and would limit its purely military activity to the raging wars in Eritrea and the Ogaden. In other words there would now be a two-pronged coordinated effort at implementing socialism: one would be purely political concentrating on domestic activity, the other would be largely military attacking those forces that either internally or externally were trying to militarily dismember Ethiopia's geographical integrity. COPWE then represented a move toward political centralization and an effort to demilitarize the socialist Ethiopian government.

COPWE is made up of a seven-member Executive Committee, and a Central Committee of 117 full and candidate members. There are fourteen Regional Committees that have a membership of between 1,500 and 2,000 members, but whose chairmen are chosen by the Executive Committee. COPWE plenary sessions, or congresses, usually meet once a year in Addis Ababa and are attended by almost 2,000 representatives. Nine separate committees exist that handle the various affairs of COPWE. In addition a newspaper, *Serto Ader* ('Working People'), is published weekly and is COPWE's attempt to educate the masses of Ethiopia. Although *Serto Ader* is directly under the authority of COPWE, both the English-language *Ethiopian Herald*, and the Amharic-language *Addis Zemen* reflect the ideology and orientation of both COPWE and the Dergue. The *Negarit Gazeta* is the official government organ that publishes all documents passed by either COPWE or the Dergue. All newspapers, as well as radio and television, act as providers of information as well as units of ideological propaganda. COPWE is a highly centralized organization that to a large degree acts as an instrument of its leadership (see Figure 6). At the same time, since auxiliary organizations include the peasant association bureaucracy, the kebelles, the All-Ethiopia Trade Union, and the Revolutionary Ethiopia's Women's Association (REWA), COPWE has to reflect to some large degree the needs of its mass membership. Thus, COPWE is in its supervisory structure an elite organization, but via its auxiliary associations it can be classified as a mass organization.

In 1984 the Dergue's influence upon COPWE is easily seen. Mengistu is chairman of COPWE and of the Dergue; the seven members of

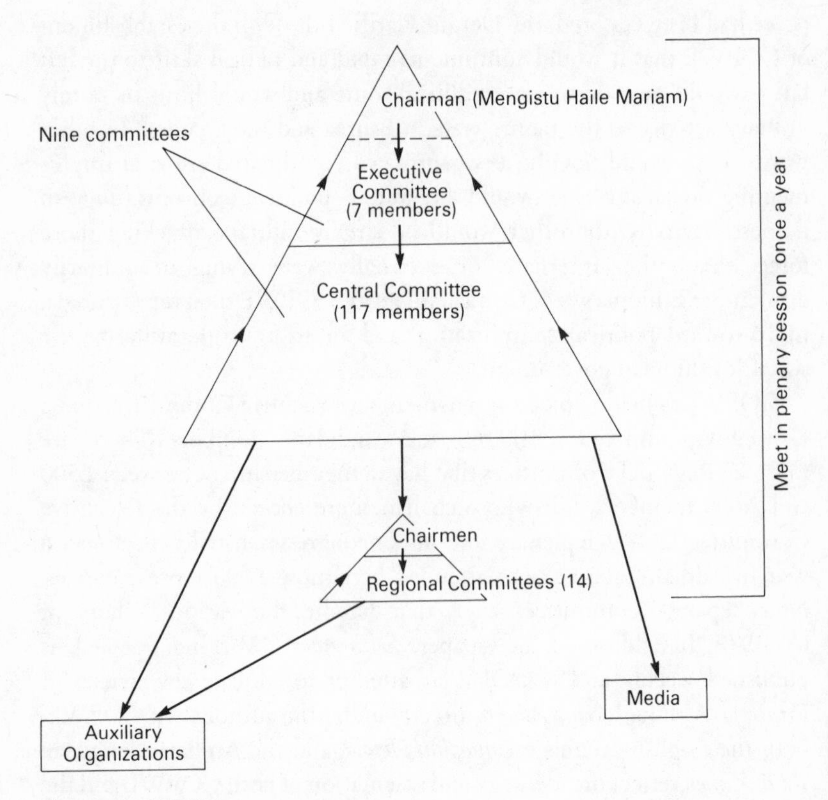

Figure 6. COPWE

COPWE's Executive Committee, headed by Mengistu, are all members of the Dergue; more than seventy-nine of the 117 full and candidate members of COPWE's Central Committee are members of the armed forces or police; all members of the Dergue's Standing Committee and Central Committee are on COPWE's Central Committee; and all fourteen of COPWE's Regional Committees are led by Dergue representatives. Essentially, 'of the COPWE Central Committee members . . . two-thirds are military' (*Swiss Review of World Affairs*, May 1981).

The leading political figures of COPWE, in addition to Mengistu, are: (a) Lt.-Col. Legesse Asfaw, of the Dergue and COPWE's Executive Committee, who received his political training in the USSR and is head of COPWE's Organization Committee; (b) Berhanu Bayih, on COPWE's

Executive Committee, an original member of the Dergue with the rank of Major, Minister of Labour and Social Affairs, in effective control of foreign affairs and who has been heavily involved in dealing with the Eritrean problem; (c) Lt.-Col. Fikre-Selassie Wogderess, pro-Soviet, a Dergue Standing Committee member and on COPWE's Executive Committee, Deputy Chairman of the Council of Ministers and head of the Ideological Committee of COPWE; (d) Brig.-Gen. Tesfaye Gebre Kidan, also pro-Soviet, of the Dergue and presently Minister of Defence; (e) Dawit Wolde Giorgis, Commissioner of Relief and Rehabilitation and on COPWE's Central Committee; (f) Goshu Wolde, Foreign Minister; (g) Addis Tedlay, representative of the air force to the Dergue and on COPWE's Executive Committee; (h) Lt.-Col. Woubshet Dessie, a Dergue member and director of COPWE's Security Committee; (i) Lt.-Col. Fisseha Desta, on COPWE's Executive and Central Committees, head of its justice and defence committees and Assistant Secretary-General of the Dergue, and less inclined towards a pro-Soviet stance; (j) Hailu Yimenu, Minister of Industry, Secretary-General of ENDRP and on COPWE's Central Committee; (k) Amanuel Amde Michael, Central Committee member and Minister of Justice; (l) Tesfaye Dinka, Minister of Finance and on COPWE's Central Committee; (m) Brig.-Gen. Seyoum Makonnen, on the Central Committee and Director of the Military Commissariat at the Ministry of Internal Administration; (n) Ashagre Yigletu, Director of the Institute for the Study of Nationalities, and on COPWE's Central Committee; (o) Gessesse Wolde Kidan, on the Dergue's Standing Committee and COPWE's Central Committee; (p) Shemelis Adugna, Director of the National Children's Commission and on the Central Committee of COPWE; (q) Col. Habte Mariam Ayenachew, Deputy Commissioner of Relief and Rehabilitation; (r) Tesfaye Habte, Central Committee member.

The intertwining of Dergue members with COPWE gives a clear indication of the military influence upon COPWE, but it should be made just as clear that Mengistu's power and control over both institutions is overwhelming. Despite the fact that no execution of any Dergue member has occurred since 1977, Mengistu's authority over other Dergue and COPWE members is crushing. Any of the major figures of COPWE can be removed from their position should Mengistu so decide. Thus both COPWE and the Dergue are structures largely under the domination of one man. On the other hand, the establishment of COPWE on 17 December 1979 clearly appears to have been Mengistu's response 'to the need for a centralizing organization and for an institution allowing civilians to play a political role without threatening the Dergue' (Ottaway, 1982, p. 142). Although civilians have a very limited role within the COPWE establishment, their influence is supported within regional congresses and within the Regional Committees. In essence COPWE's leadership is slowly guiding Ethiopia toward a centralized system that is militarily dominated, but that via its sub-organizations is decentralized and civilian orientated. COPWE then is a dual pre-party system. Decision-making comes from above by the self-same Dergue leaders who radicalized Ethiopia and pushed hard for the implantation of socialism. Although military influence is vivid, there is room for civilian participation. Although this system cannot be termed democratic, it can be characterized as one that continues the process of legitimizing socialism in Ethiopia through a highly centralized form of pre-party organization that has within it the rudiments of socialist democracy.

Besides being responsible for organizing a vanguard political party and dealing with the issue of class formation COPWE, in alliance with the Dergue, is in charge of developing the ideological parameters of the state and is also responsible for the affairs of state. It is in the latter two areas that real problems of policy-making and organization exist. As centralized as the political order is, lines of political and bureaucratic responsibility are blurred, and it is difficult for those who fill roles in the Dergue, COPWE and the government bureaucracy, to decide where their political territory begins and ends. Although the creation of COPWE was an important milestone in the shift towards a civilian revolution, the three structures compete to a large degree. At the same time, since almost all power and authority rests with the Dergue and COPWE, the ministries of government responsible for the day-to-day running of Ethiopia have very limited authority. As a result individuals in these ministries, who are not ranking members of COPWE or the Dergue, try to avoid as much as possible making any decisions or giving any solid advice for fear of running foul of either COPWE or the Dergue. Clearly, the bureaucracy has an uneasy relationship with the power centres. Paul H. Brietzke has described the political confusion perfectly.

> The Dergue's . . . approach to administration involved the assignment of a soldier—usually young, inexperienced, and often poorly educated—to supervise each senior administrator. . . . These soldiers often take pleasure in countermanding the decisions of senior bureaucrats, or lack the self-confidence to approve any course of action. Later [COPWE members also began to supervise administrators]. In theory, members of a 'troika' . . . function as equals in each agency, but the Dergue's man usually dominates. [1982, p. 201.]

The inefficiency and lethargy that results is not so very different from that which existed under Haile Selassie's government. The ability of government ministries to function is hampered by fear and a clear lack of authority.

This problem is exacerbated by structural replication of responsibility and by competing areas of responsibility intrastructurally. Berhanu Bayih, for instance, plays a key role in determining foreign policy, and is a member both of COPWE and the Dergue. Goshu Wolde is Foreign Minister and thus theoretically both advances and carries out foreign policy. Are decisions made within the Dergue, COPWE, or the ministry? And who has the primary responsibility for foreign policy? To put it a bit differently, what role does each structure have in the making of decisions, and how far does the responsibility of the key political actors extend in terms of how decisions are made? What is clearly lacking is precision in terms of lines of responsibility, both structurally and personally. On paper as well as in practice the lines are unclear. The primary question then is: when there is a difference of opinion, which structure has the real power and which individuals wield the greatest influence?

To some degree a tentative answer can be given. Since the Dergue is so inter-related with COPWE and still maintains an independent political existence, its authority is presumably primary. If the Dergue had fully integrated itself with COPWE then COPWE would clearly have been the supreme political force. The only reason that the Dergue continued as a political entity after the creation of COPWE was so that it could persist in guiding and influencing the political direction of Ethiopia. The government ministries in Ethiopia have traditionally been relatively powerless and there is no evidence to show that the situation is otherwise at the present time. Their primary function is to carry out Dergue or COPWE edicts, and to deal with relatively innocuous day-to-day matters. They may, as in any bureaucracy, pace the carrying out of decisions or influence their tone and style, but they play almost no role in establishing policy or influencing ideology. Despite the fact then, that placing the Dergue within the confines of COPWE via its personnel, and maintaining its autonomy was innovative, in practice the Dergue remains the central political structure. COPWE has the ability to influence, but it is the Dergue that holds the power and wields it through its own structures and COPWE.

As for who holds power in Ethiopia the answer is clear: without question it is Mengistu. Together with the pro-Soviet core of Legesse Asfaw, Berhanu Bayih, Fikre-Selassie Wogderess and Tesfaye Gebre Kidan, he dominates the Dergue, COPWE and the government bureaucracy. The political centre is the Dergue and the centre of the Dergue is Mengistu. Individuals in the highly centralized political system are powerful and influential only in so far as authority is bestowed upon them by Mengistu. Thus it would be Berhanu rather than Goshu who dominates in the area of foreign affairs despite the latter's position as foreign minister; and although Berhanu has played a prominent role in the revolution, should Mengistu so decide, his power could be sharply curtailed. In essence the only political constituency that counts is Mengistu. This is so despite the fact that he decided it was important to begin the process of institutionalizing the revolution. His role may be altered in the future, but it is doubtful that he would voluntarily step down or severely curtail his own authority. At the moment his concern is to stabilize the revolution, organize it, and direct it toward a socialist construct. Mengistu then rules Ethiopia predominately through the Dergue, along with Dergue members, many of whom are Amhara (according to the *Ethiopian Herald*, 25 June 1980, two-thirds of COPWE's Central Committee is made up of Amhara). The power of these members is wholly a function of their loyalty to Mengistu. Even the anti-Dergue journal *Ethiopia Profile* acknowledged Mengistu's role in attaining loyalty and stabilizing and civilianizing the revolution.

> It is now more than eight years since the military took over in Ethiopia. . . . Be it by design or sheer luck, Mengistu has proved to date to be a very skilful operator. His . . . alliances . . ., his success in organizing . . . COPWE . . . stand out clearly as his personal achievements. . . . [December 1982, p. 10.]

The Dergue then rules together with COPWE although the latter is in an inferior political position. Some devolution of authority from the Dergue to COPWE has taken place, but on a limited basis. COPWE was created to begin the process of moving towards a civilian and a political orientation, and is only in its early stages. Thus more transference of power from the Dergue to COPWE may take place in the future with, perhaps, the soldiers taking off their uniforms and moving the Dergue fully within COPWE. On the other hand both may co-exist until a real vanguard party is created to lead Ethiopia to communism. But until either takes place there will continue to be control by the centre, but in a loose rather disorganized fashion that may lead to factionalism and poor socialist direction. Although Mengistu has thus far been extremely effective in charting Ethiopia along a socialist path, it would appear important now to cohere the political centre into a more disciplined and organized instrument (see Figure 7).

Three other important areas that may provoke conflict within the centre are (1) the issue of Amhara chauvinism and domination, (2) the pro-Soviet versus the nationalist faction, and (3) rivalry among the central leadership.These are potentially far more dangerous than the merely administrative lack of coherence because they are less easily solved.

It is clear that the Amhara are once again represented in central officialdom far out of proportion to their numbers in society as a whole. In and of itself this may be meaningless; but given the historical tradition of Ethiopia the perception is as important as the reality. It must be made clear to the population that despite their numbers they wield no undue influence. In 1977 when Somalia invaded the Ogaden, Haile Fida opposed the Dergue policy of arming the old Amhara settlers of the south, claiming that it was a step backward for the revolution. This was one of the issues that caused the split between the Dergue and *Me'ison*, that eventually led Mengistu to arrest Haile. One could hardly describe the arming of these men in an attempt to preserve Ethiopia's territorial integrity as regression of the revolution and rehabilitation of the old guard, but the anti-Amhara sentiment in Ethiopia is so strong that every attempt must be made not to permit their re-emergence into the power centres to go without official comment. It must be transmitted to the population by Mengistu that individuals are in the arena of authority because of their talents and politics, not because of their ethnicity. If the Dergue and COPWE are seen as too conciliatory to the once-oppressive Amhara (as it seems they currently are, Halliday & Molyneux, 1981,

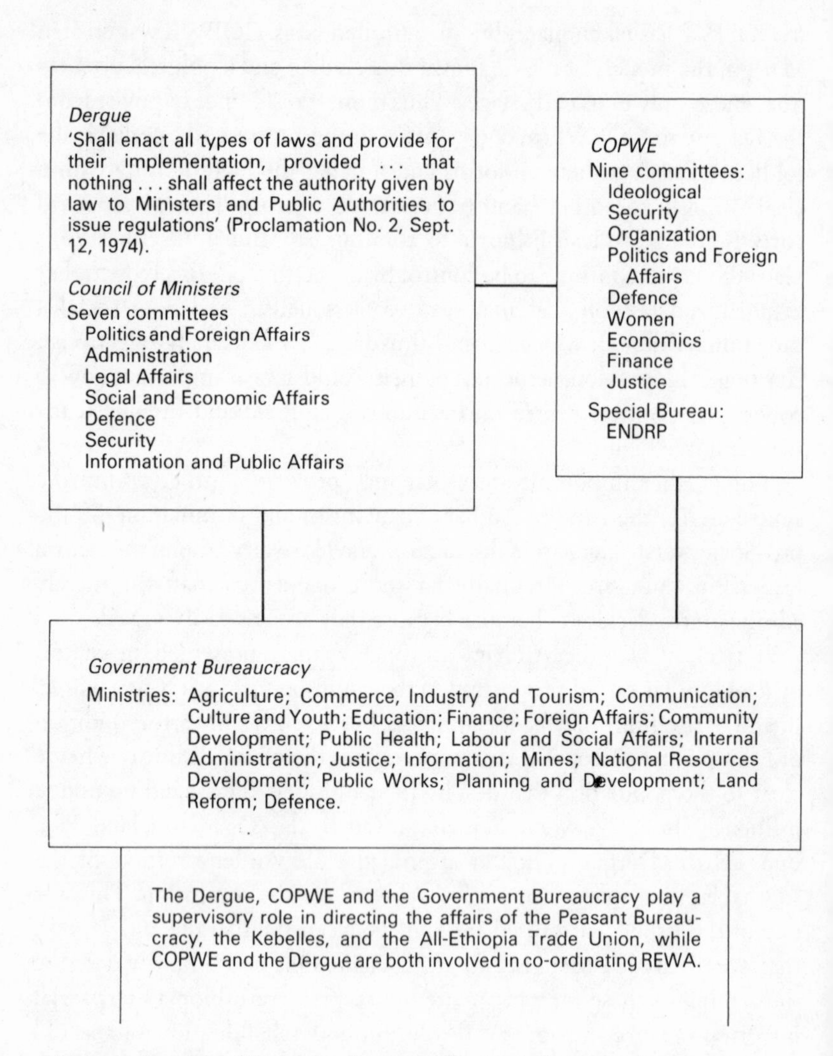

Figure 7. Socialist Ethiopia: Overlapping Political Jurisdictions—The Centre

p. 165) it could lead to upheavals against the socialist government. It is important for Mengistu not only to speak on the subject, but to ensure that the Amhara do not re-emerge as the primary political actors solely because of their ethnicity. If this were to occur it would violate the ideals of the revolution and Lenin's thesis that ethnic distinctions must be obliterated. Of all the areas of potential conflict this may well be the most serious, and therefore it must be confronted in the most political and responsible manner. If the Amhara representatives in the Dergue and COPWE continue to dominate, then a policy statement must be issued that emphasizes their value to the state and reduces the importance of their ethnic composition. Ethnicity is not important in a socialist revolution and should not be, but it must not be seen by the people to be important, otherwise there is certain to be trouble. This is a sensitive issue but it must be confronted. Finally, it must be asked why the Amhara are so heavily weighted in positions of authority. Ethiopia is a mix of ethnic groups, and the most numerous of them are right to be sensitive to the issue of Amhara domination. Such an explosive issue, and one that has not really been dealt with *vis-à-vis* the public has to be of concern to decision makers, and if it is not one must ask why. It is vital for the future of the revolution that this question be settled.

Leadership rivalry is most likely to occur over the issue of pro-Soviet sentiment. Mengistu is trying to preserve a close political connection with the Soviets while also attempting to maintain some distance, so as not to allow Ethiopia to become overwhelmed by the relationship. In 1978 Ethiopia signed a Treaty of Friendship and Cooperation with the Soviet Union, and its military forces have been heavily armed by the Soviets since that time. But 'the limits of the Soviet influence in Ethiopia are best revealed by the fact that the USSR did not obtain much for itself' despite arming Ethiopia to the tune of over $2 billion, and 'even politically the Soviet Union has not derived any tangible benefits from its relation with Ethiopia' (Ottaway, 1982, pp. 149, 151). Although this assertion may be disputed (see below), it is clear that Ethiopia's ties to the Soviet Union are either closer or more distant than some of the Dergue leaders would like to see, and it is over this issue that a leadership crisis might arise. Certainly post-revolutionary Egypt and Cuba pose radically different alternatives to the Ethiopian leadership.

Pro-Soviet versus nationalist sentiment is apparently of some consequence currently. It is a point of discussion in Ottaway (1982) and Halliday & Molyneux (1981), and has been the focus of a study by *Ethiopia Profile* (December 1982, p. 14), which concluded that

It is also an expression of a very strong rejection of any further closeness to Moscow that people like Legesse Asfaw are purported to be pushing. If there is any post-revolutionary consciousness in Ethiopia that is clearly detectable, it is the rejection of continued subservience to Moscow and of the surrender of sovereignty.

Whether Ethiopia ties itself more into the international web of communist theory, as Lenin demanded, or shifts to a more nationalist perspective is an issue that is likely to gain pertinence with the solidifying of socialism. The issue may be resolved by the re-institution of violence and the settlement of disputes via the gun, or it may be dealt with through negotiation and discussion. If the issue is allowed to fester it could severely detract from the ongoing socialist revolution and perhaps destroy some of the extraordinary gains that have already been made.

Finally, leadership conflict might arise over Dergue and COPWE leaders trying 'to prove themselves more committed to Mengistu than to the "revolution". In their ardour to prove such loyalty, some have gone to the extent of mystifying the person of Mengistu in much the same manner as with the late Emperor' (ibid., pp. 10, 14). The cult of personality doctrine must be avoided at all costs. Loyalty based on acceptance of the prevailing theoretical ideology is one thing, but to have it predicated merely on sycophancy would substitute personalism for ideology and politics, and would destroy the genuine fabric of the revolution. To use Lenin's term this would be 'opportunism' leading 'to most deplorable consequences' (Lenin, in Mazlish, 1971, p. 150).

Although problems with the centre persist, the centralization of the state, within a political framework, was advanced by the establishment of COPWE. At the same time, through an original and innovative procedure, the higher level participants in the Dergue continued to maintain their role as the primary advocates of the transition to socialism. The Dergue and COPWE now share in the position of vanguard of the revolution and together are moving to mobilize many more millions of Ethiopians into the political order. Essentially, they form a political/military dynamic that represents an increasingly centralized and institutionalized political system. At the pinnacle sits Mengistu, yet with all his power he has conformed to the thesis of Lenin that a vanguard structure must be created and nurtured, so that it in time will play the paramount political role. It would appear that whatever Mengistu's personal stake in the political structure, he is astutely and quickly organizing the socialist edifice of the state. He has moved Ethiopia rapidly and intelligently into the political orbit of socialism. When one considers that prior to 1974 socialism was not part of any group's ideology, was virtually forbidden to exist, and that its validity was generally denied throughout feudal Ethiopia, one understands the turmoil that society had to go through to reach its relatively original stage of socialist construction. The strengthening of the central apparatus from 1979 on is an important aspect of Ethiopia's development towards socialist orthodoxy.

Auxiliary Structures

Peasant Association Bureaucracy

The radical land distribution programme entails a number of contradictions difficult to resolve. Despite the fact that upwards of eleven million peasants are incorporated within the All-Ethiopian Peasant Association and that land reform has had marked political success as discussed above, political and geographical limitations exist that hamper the connection between the centre and the peasant associations.

Perhaps the most intractable problem is the small number of primary roads, the terribly poor condition of the road network in general, and the small number of people that live near any road whatsoever. The ability of either the central government or the Central Planning Supreme Council to reach people and then to ensure that redistribution of land takes place as required is therefore severely restricted. In this case the ideology of socialist Ethiopia is beside the point. The state faces the same dilemma as the Haile Selassie government: it cannot reach many of its people, and as a result traditional values and political forces wield greater authority in those unreachable interior areas. 'Bale, Gemu Goffa, and Illubabor have no all-weather roads and Wallega has only 80 kilometers of such roads. . . . Most of the terrain in Ethiopia . . . is rugged and makes . . . construction of roads . . . difficult . . .' (Bequele & Chole, 1969, pp. 91, 93). The political difficulties resulting from the state's inability to reach much of its population requires no lengthy discussion. It is clear that if the central political order is to have universal control over land reform, it will have to develop a road transportation grid that will give it the ability effectively to connect to its interior population. More developmental aid and allocation of monies must be considered. Anyone who travels in Ethiopia will verify that the road network is no better now than it was when Bequele and Chole wrote their analysis. Although the Dergue and COPWE are clearly aware of this problem, they have been unable to deal with it adequately because of the need to concentrate on acquiring military aid due to the situation in the Ogaden and Eritrea. But with the stabilizing of both these areas, the state will now have to extend its efforts in making more or less the entire country accessible to the centre.

An issue of political consequence relates to class distinctions within the peasantry. Although this is not a major contradiction, in the coffee growing areas of the country 'the richer peasants were able . . . to gain a disproportionate amount of the land [and] also to ensure that it was they who controlled the new Peasant Associations' (Halliday & Molyneux, 1981, p. 108). In addition despite 'the existence of a state purchasing board for coffeee, the sale of [this] commodity remained to a considerable extent in the hands of the same powerful merchants who had controlled it in the days of Haile Selassie' (ibid., p. 111). Understandable as it is that the Dergue desired to maintain coffee production and did not want to disrupt production by enforcing land reform in these areas, in this case the politics of land reform enforcement must take priority over the economics of it. There cannot be backtracking that entails the continuance of class distinctions which could easily lead to a subversion of class formation that both the Dergue and COPWE are presently charged with ensuring. The National Revolution Development Campaign must see that distribution takes place equitably and without consideration of class background. Establishing facilities that will train peasants in coffee production, and setting up political centres that can re-educate once-prosperous and private farmers into the new political order can go far in resolving this contradiction. Excuses can always be given that the economy must take precedence over politics, but if the solutions above are enacted there will be no antagonism between economics and politics.

As analysed earlier, land reform has gone far in ensuring that socialism in Ethiopia will be implemented. Its success has been extraordinary, particularly on the political level. Overall, the peasant bureaucracy has performed notably in securing the success of land distribution. It is true however that there are contradictions that limit the effectiveness of its overall implementation. They are also reinforced by the enormous numbers of people involved in the programme. With millions under the rubric of the peasant associations, and with many of them distant and inaccessible, it has been virtually impossible for the centre and the peasant structures to ensure absolute equity. The Dergue and COPWE should now iron out the political and geographical seams of land reform so that the only problems are the natural ones due to the enormous numbers of people involved. This however is a problem rather than a contradiction. There appears no reason other than a lack of funds why the state cannot resolve the unevenness of land reform. And with peace being basically restored throughout the country, funding is not really an insurmountable issue any more. The state is now in a position to complete its land reform programme.

Kebelles

The decentralized nature of the peasant associations dictated by geography and numbers of people spread throughout the country is a complexity that does not apply to the kebelles. Discussed at length above, the kebelles remain tightly tied to the central political organs of the state, despite the fact that they have autonomous and independent social and political responsibility. They cannot diverge from the directives issued by the state, and basically they respond to the centre. Although they have much authority over the citizenry attached to kebelles, and the populace remains accountable in its everyday affairs to them, their relationship to the centre is overwhelming and inferior. At the same time their proximity in all urban areas permits the centre to know more concretely what is going on within their domain. Thus the contradictions and limitations of the centre that apply to the peasant structures are not apparent within the kebelles. As part of the policy of decentralizing the central administration, the kebelles have operated very successfully. They have indeed incorporated the urban proletariat and petty bourgeoisie into the revolution, and have extended into the farthest reaches of each neighbourhood. Although kebelles have in the past overreached their authority they, to a very large degree, no longer do so. Kebelles, then, have proved their value as a judicial, social and political instrument of the state. They have also enforced the urban houses proclamation thereby playing an important role in the redistribution of wealth from one class to another. The kebelles remain a formative political organ.

All-Ethiopia Trade Union

Although the All-Ethiopia Trade Union is closely tied to the centre, it is very much an auxiliary structure in the same way that the kebelles are. Though centre-oriented, the All-Ethiopia Trade Union reaches into urban and township sectors supervising the labour movement in accordance with socialist values. The AETU was created in 1977 to replace the rather conservative CELU which was established in the 1960s because of pressure placed on Haile Selassie by Western trade unions and by the United States. In an effort to appease these powerful entities the emperor allowed the creation of CELU, but maintained strict control over it; CELU itself viewed its role primarily as a 'mutual aid association' (see Ottaway & Ottaway, 1978, p. 23, and Ottaway, 1976). By 1974 it had a membership of over 80,000, was primarily white-collar, and was concerned with the economic improvement of its membership. During the early months of the revolution CELU tried to pass itself off as a radical entity that sympathized with the ideals of the Dergue but differed in its tactics. CELU was involved in promoting economic reforms, but it could hardly be called radical or socialist. Its white-collar petty bourgeois and proletariat base along with its Western affiliation defined its real domestically conservative and internationally liberal politics. It finally broke with the Dergue when the latter moved to the left, and used tactics that differed sharply with how CELU viewed the revolution should move (Ottaway, 1976). Its hierarchy was imprisoned or executed and AETU was established to replace it.

Predicated on the 1975 Labour Proclamation, AETU is a 'super' union constituted of all industry-wide unions. All unions have compulsory membership in AETU. Although the AETU has the economic betterment of its members as its goal (see Labour Proclamation, 1975, and Brietzke, 1982, pp. 280-6) its primary role is as a political structure. The leadership of the union, in practice appointed by the Dergue and COPWE, is accountable to the general assembly elected by the multiple number of unions represented in AETU. But all decisions and recommendations to the centre must help to build socialism and must strictly observe socialist legality (Labour Proclamation, 1975).

In its early years AETU was caught up in the fires of revolution that were spreading throughout Ethiopia. The EPRP assassinated its first three chairmen, and *Me'ison*, which at that time dominated AETU, tried to use it to establish a civilian government, thus leading to a purge of its membership and the arrest of Haile Fida by the Dergue. By 1981 labour and political discipline had been re-established and membership was reported to be over 400,000 (*Africa Confidential*, 11 March, 1981).

Presently AETU is primarily a political organ of the state. Although it has achieved improvement in wages and benefits for its members and ensures that unfair labour practices are dealt with, the state has, as Markakis and Ayele claim, reduced 'the organized labour movement to the status of a state agency' (Markakis & Ayele, 1978, p. 186). But if one analyses the position of AETU within a socialist vanguard perspective it is clear that AETU is basically utilized to ensure that socialist values are disseminated through and to the urban proletariat. With AETU wage-earners having been engulfed in a political maelstrom from 1974 to 1981 it is important that through the kebelles and AETU the urban sector's political and economic values are joined with the needs of a state that is presently in the transition stage to socialism. Through an auxiliary structure (AETU) that is closely intertwined with the centre, the proletariat can be socialized to see that socialist values are in tune with their own needs and hopes. This is precisely the role that AETU was established to accomplish. Once the values of the workers are more in accord with socialist values, the position of AETU may become more autonomous and powerful. Until that time, however, AETU will continue, first and foremost, as a political instrument.

Revolutionary Ethiopia's Women's Association

REWA was organized in July 1980 so as to coordinate the many women's associations that were created as part of the kebelles, factories and peasant associations. Until 1980 each women's association acted for itself within other structures, even though most were revolutionary and opted for socialist values. But since both the EPRP and *Me'ison* opposed their feminist first, class second perspective, and then tried to take them over for their own political ends, the Dergue and COPWE moved to incorporate all women's associations under one rubric. Prior to 1980 all women's associations functioned as part of a kebelle, factory or peasant association, but held a status independent of them; so they worked with these structures but were separate from them. REWA was also an attempt to deal with this social confusion. Under REWA class rather than sex was seen as the primary force of oppression (which adhered to the Soviet line), and women's associations worked more in line with the kebelles, factories and peasant associations. Still, the integration was never to be total, and even under REWA women's associations retain a status of limited independence.

The revolution had a tremendous impact on the position of women. Under Haile Selassie, Addis Ababa was known as the prostitution capital of the Third World. The mayor of Addis Ababa maintained in 1977 that in his city upwards of 100,000 women were engaged in prostitution (Halliday & Molyneux, 1981, p. 144). In addition male dominance of the family structure was total. At times of famine women and little girls were always fed last, thus ensuring that the highest death rate at such times applied to females (for more on male dominance see Levine, 1965). Commenting on the changes wrought by the revolution, Sthaye, organizer of the Addis Ababa-based Akaki Women's Association, maintained in 1978:

> After the land reform it was much easier to organize the women. When the rich families owned the land, women weren't allowed to till the fields. . . . Since they got a percentage of the crop, the landlords only wanted strong men working the fields, so if the husband died the women had to leave and become either servants, beggars, or prostitutes. But with the land reform every family, whether it be headed by a man or a woman, got the same amount of land to work.
>
> It was even harder for the factory women. They had to work all day and then come home and do all the housework too—the men wouldn't take the responsibility. Now through the women's associations in the kebelles and factories, we are trying to solve this. [Griswold, 1978b, pp. 31, 32-3.]

Or, as the leader of the Arssi Women's Association in Arusi Region stated, 'we oppressed women are also conducting our class struggle' (ibid., p. 12).

Even before the creation of REWA, women benefited in an extraordinary way from the revolution. Their consciousness raised, they demanded and worked for, within their association, equality in the rural and urban settings. For many, the rope that had held them by the neck for centuries had been cut and permitted women to articulate their demands. Although rural women had a far more difficult time doing so because of customary and traditional values, the establishment of peasant associations supported the changing position of women. REWA reinforced the new role of women even more as it gave central ideological approval, through a political structure, of women's role in the revolution. REWA acts in an auxiliary fashion via its decentralized structure, and influences policy at the centre as well as ensuring that central directives are carried out in the regions.

Feudal Ethiopia had been horribly oppressive to women for centuries and the repression was unrelenting. In 1974 the revolution brought to women a degree of freedom they had never before experienced. REWA is meant to ensure, stabilize and legitimize that liberty.

All four auxiliary structures—the peasant association bureaucracy, kebelles, the All-Ethiopia Trade Union, and Revolutionary Ethiopia's Women's Association—are not directly part of the centre, but are tied to it very closely. They function as adjuncts of the centre but they are rather decentralized. Their role is to carry through directives from the centre as well as pass data and information to the central political organs. They are important political units of the revolution, and in fact they are those structures that do most in carrying the revolution to the people. To a large degree they are innovative and vital to the success of the revolution (see Figure 8).

Political Dissent

Ten years after the revolution, political dissent and opposition to the socialist state have been almost quashed. *Me'ison* and the EPRP were eliminated in the late 1970s and their membership was forced into exile, shot, or imprisoned. Those who are still alive and free in Ethiopia have been forced through politics and violence to drop any direct participation in the outlawed organizations. The EDU, originally composed of remnants of the former landed aristocracy, was never very successful, and in its limited military confrontations with the forces of the Dergue in the 1970s it was overwhelmed. Most of the old EDU leadership in Ethiopia were killed, while others vanished into obscurity in London. Three organizational spin-offs from the EDU appeared between 1977 and 1981, each of which reflected the original EDU, led by Gen. Iyassu Mengesha, Ras Mengesha Seyum, Gen. Nega Tegene, Fesha Jammo and Tellela Hailu. The new organizations, the Popular Ethiopian Democratic Union (PEDU), formed in 1977 in the Sudan by Commodore Tasew, Iyasus

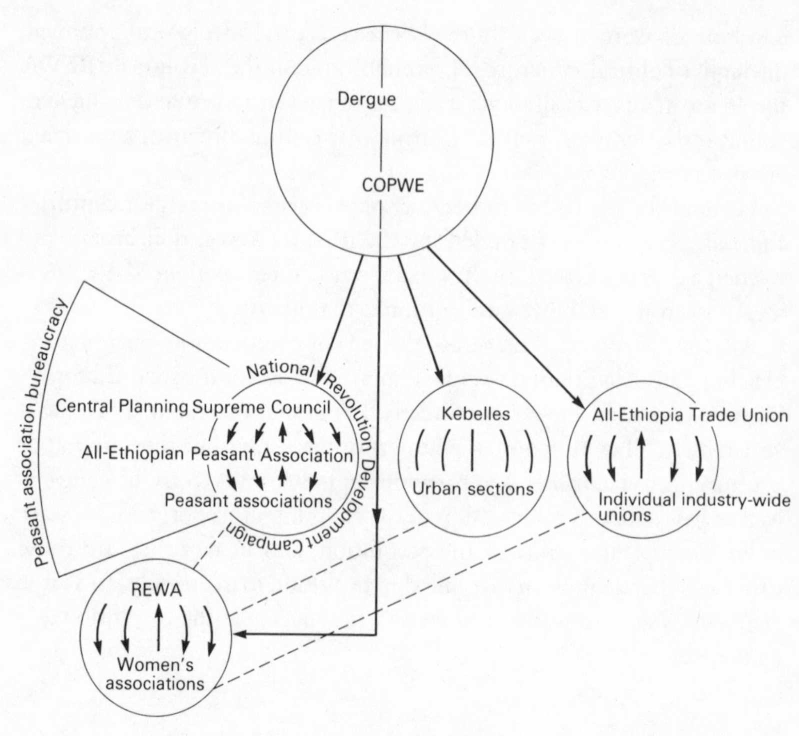

Figure 8. Auxiliary Structures (and their connection to the centre)

Worq Zafu, and Fekare Gabre Kal; the Ethiopian People's Democratic Revolutionary Party (EPDRP), also created in 1977, and the Democratic Front for the Liberation of Ethiopia (DFLE), set up in 1981, had virtually no membership and were essentially paper organizations. Sultan Ali Mirreh Hanafare, of the ALF, fled in 1975 to Saudi Arabia after the ALF had been routed by the Dergue. Whatever was left of the organization was absorbed by the EDU. Periodically Afar bands attack Ethiopian troops. The Ethiopian People's Democratic Movement (EPDM), and the Democratic Socialist Party of Ethiopia (DSPE), both organized in 1982, are centrist groups that also exist almost solely on paper. The Tigre Liberation Movement (TLM) organized in 1974, also by Ras Mengesha Seyum, continues to fight against COPWE and the Dergue, and together with the left-oriented Tigre Popular Liberation Front (TPLF) causes periodic military confrontations with the state in Tigre. TLM desires a more liberal state while the

TPLF, organized in 1975, advocates secession. Growing in power, both have deep popular support that at the present time is underground because of the Dergue's crushing military policy in the north. The only internal opposition that has been pronounced *and* has come close to achieving its goals exists in Eritrea and in the Ogaden. Secessionist movements in both areas forced the socialist state into a military posture in the late 1970s that pushed Ethiopia more securely into the Soviet bloc camp. (This will be discussed at length in Chapter 4.)

Within Ethiopia no effective organized opposition exists, and none is permitted to exist. The Dergue, through its violent tactics early on, has cleared Ethiopia of all oppositional groups; unafraid to use overwhelmingly deadly force, opposing forces have been terrorized out of existence, and if they exist at all they usually are set up out of the country and thus have limited internal support. In 1984 Ethiopia is cleansed of opponents and everyday life is peaceful and largely nonviolent. It must also be emphasized that all indications are that the policies of the state have generated wide-ranging support from both the urban and rural population, and as a result oppositional organizations would find it difficult in any case to attract supporters. What was said about DSPE by *Ethiopia Profile* (April 1982, p. 4) sums up what can be said about all opposition forces inside Ethiopia: 'but then DSPE may prove to be only ephemeral and there is little need to dwell on it longer.' *Ethiopia Profile*'s analysis of EPRP (ibid., p. 12) also reflects the reality of the impact of groups organized to oppose the socialist state: 'the surviving [members] remain . . . a miniscule group that [have] no significant impact or influence in the contemporary situation.'

Although political dissent within Ethiopia has become almost irrelevant, intellectual dissent outside the country has been vocal, although clearly ineffective. The reference here is to Ethiopian scholars who, though as a group were largely opposed to the oppression and cruelty of the Haile Selassie government, could not abide the violence attached to the Dergue and its refusal to incorporate into the revolution the more 'purist' Marxist ideology advocated in particular by the students. Ethiopianists, who once favoured radical change, questioned the reasonableness of the Dergue's policies, thus moving in their writings to condemn the Dergue. Markakis and Ayele summed up this attitude when they maintained (1978, p. 119)

> The wanton manner of the executions . . . shocked many Ethiopians. The executions marked a new stage in the revolution and a crossing point for the Dergue. The

revolution is no longer bloodless, and ruthlessness increasingly marks its course from now on.

Almost all prominent Ethiopianists at one time or another came out against the Dergue in their publications. They have been either unwilling or unable to accept (1) the violence imposed by the Dergue, (2) socialism implanted by a military elite, (3) the lack of traditional progress towards socialism, or (4) socialism itself. Only Marina and David Ottaway, Fred Halliday and Maxine Molyneux, and this author, among reputed Ethiopianists, have seen the revolution as a positive step despite some of the excesses. Basically, the one group has identified the excesses as the hallmark of the revolution, while the other has seen them merely as a political weapon or as an unfortunate by-product. Because the number of Ethiopianists is small and influential within academic and intellectual circles, their ability to sway interpretations of the revolution is marked. Although ineffectual in altering events in Ethiopia, Ethiopianists play a fairly substantial role in the moulding of public opinion among intellectual and international circles. It is unfortunate that so many Ethiopianists have miscalculated in their analysis of the revolution.

Opposition that is in exile has been most vocal in its condemnation of the Ethiopian state. This is particularly so in the United States where some 30,000 students, many of them Eritreans or former members of EPRP, reside. A large majority of this number are enrolled in colleges and universities in New York City and Washington, D.C., where *ad hoc* groups have sprung up clamouring for independence for Eritrea and/or removal of the Ethiopian government. What is so ironic about their insistence for 'democracy' in Ethiopia 'is that many of these individuals were the same persons who held positions of dominance prior to the revolution, who held tenant-farmers at their mercy, and who lived off the fruits of oppression' (Schwab, 1982, p. 198). Thus their claims are somewhat hollow. In 1982 US President Ronald Reagan proclaimed that since Ethiopia was stabilized, a policy of returning the exiles to the country would be put in force. Despite the fact that the Ethiopian embassy in Washington, D.C. claimed that many of the exiles held skills that would be welcomed in an Ethiopia that was no longer at war with itself, the refugees refused even to consider the offer. Instead, the exiles together with Amnesty International, the Phelps Stokes Fund, Cultural Survival and the Democratic

Socialists of America held forums in an attempt to sway the US Congress into passing legislation that would allow them to remain in the United States. Although this effort failed, the Reagan Administration did not push the issue, and only a small number of Ethiopians were expelled from the United States.

One effect of Reagan's policy, however, was to still the Ethiopian student movement in the United States. With the United States in 1982-3 in the midst of an economic recession with unemployment surpassing 10 per cent, the students were fearful of igniting once again a policy that was predicated on limiting foreign populations in the United States that were seen as taking jobs away from Americans. So, the Ethiopian student movement became silent organizationally. Although the students never had any power to alter events inside Ethiopia, the Ethiopian government, which was seriously trying to increase its economic aid from the West, felt the students in exile were undermining this policy. But, in fact the government never had to worry. Anyone attending any of the meetings or conferences put on by the various student organizations could see that these 'left' groups spent such time fighting themselves verbally and organizationally that they could never act in any unified fashion to lobby against Ethiopia in the United States. They were involved in internecine struggles that made them politically unimportant and irrelevant. It is hard to see how anyone could ever have taken their politics seriously. Caught up in personal contradictions and political in-fighting, this was an oppositional group in name only. And exiled student activities indicated very strongly that it was only the Dergue/COPWE that understood what the position and platform of the left in Ethiopia had to be. They were implementing that policy while opposition groups of the left were battling amongst themselves or had disappeared.

One group of exiles however has not dropped out of the picture. In 1978 the Journal *Horn of Africa* began publication followed in 1982 by *Ethiopia Profile*. Both are anti-Dergue and oppose the values and tactics of the Ethiopian state. Although *Horn of Africa* claims to be 'an independent Journal', among its editors are Ethiopian students who fled the country, and former government officials who served either Haile Selassie or the present government with which they became disenchanted. In addition intellectuals from the Sudan and Somalia also serve on the editorial board and display the same anti-Ethiopian government assumptions. *Ethiopia*

Profile also maintains that it is an independent 'monthly Journal of news, views and reviews'. It, however, refuses to publish the list of its editors and organizers, and virtually every issue has within it an attack on the Ethiopian polity. It is clear that *Horn of Africa*, published in the United States, and *Ethiopia Profile*, published in London, serve as the major organs for the intellectuals within the exile community that are intent on countering the present Ethiopian political order. Both are primarily propaganda publications that ought not to present themselves as objective. Although important and solidly good articles can be found in each, it is evident that both journals offer intellectual refuge for those exiles that want a place to articulate their opposition to the Dergue/COPWE. Although this is perfectly sound the journals ought to admit and publicize their political views. Still, both are effective publications in relation to presenting exile views that differ extensively from the policies of socialist Ethiopia.

Organized and effective opposition to the state, however, does not exist. Since the Dergue early on in the revolution captured the support of the population, dissenting groups have been hard put to attract adherents. Those groups that once did exist were fairly easily eliminated since they operated very much in isolation from society and often from reality. Wherever organized opposition prevails it is outside of Ethiopia and carries no weight inside the country.

Anomic opposition does occur intermittently within Ethiopia. Bands from one organization or another frequently attack squads of Ethiopian troops. Also, groups of farmers will periodically rebel against further imposition of land reform decrees. It has happened in Gojjam and in Sidamo, both of which have had a history of such rebellious activity (see Schwab, 1972, chs 8, 9). But such activity is neither serious nor extensive.

Overall, then, Ethiopia is now generally free from oppositional tendencies. Even in Eritrea and the Ogaden, where opposition was once both organized and powerful, relative calm has been restored, and the opposition has been essentially destroyed. Political dissent has been muted.

Future Prospects

Ethiopia's political system is, in 1984, at the stage where it can move in a number of directions. It may shift directly to a vanguard party structure that will replace both COPWE and the Dergue; the present structure might be maintained indefinitely; or the Dergue may very well integrate itself within COPWE, maintaining the latter as a pre-party organism until such time that it decides a vanguard party is essential to the establishment of true socialism in Ethiopia. If, as now appears unlikely, opposition to the government grows, the Dergue could abolish COPWE and return to ruling Ethiopia alone. On the other hand, it is not out of the question that the internal dynamic within the Dergue may propel another group of officers to move against Mengistu and take power. This may occur as a result of either pro- or anti-Soviet sentiment. The most likely scenario, however, is one that includes the creation of a vanguard political structure to succeed either COPWE or the present Dergue/COPWE alliance. There have been persistent official reports that such an alternative is currently being considered and planned for by Mengistu and his aides (see *Ethiopia Profile*, December 1982, p. 10 and *1984 Yearbook on International Communist Affairs*). Both theoretically and practically Ethiopia is at the stage where a vanguard party ought to be created: it would abide by Lenin's thesis that a vanguard party is the only proper mechanism through which to bring about and solidify socialism; and with the present vacuum of oppositional tendencies Ethiopia could create such an entity comfortable in the knowledge that support for Dergue/COPWE could, with relative ease, be transferred to the new party. With the political order having been stabilized by 1984, there does not appear to be a more propitious time for the installation of a vanguard political party. Dergue/COPWE ought surely to move in that direction. Mengistu is looking to 12 September 1984, the tenth anniversary of the Dergue's official move into the power structure; there has, in fact, been an official statement that the Second Congress of COPWE has approved just such a proposal (Addis Ababa Domestic Service, 25 March 1983). Dergue and COPWE would be moving far in institutionalizing socialism in Ethiopia, if it rapidly acted to create a party. Unless some major unforeseen event occurs disrupting the present evolution toward socialism, it can be expected that in one form or another such a vanguard party will be established. Ethiopia will then have integrated its originality with orthodoxy, will have moved further to the left, and will have established itself as the first socialist state to have done so via the auspices of a military vanguard. Ethiopia's socialist order has come very far since 1974; it is now appropriate that it move to a more lasting structural arrangement so that the position of socialism can be more assured.

And finally there is the issue of political democracy. It has up to now been necessary, because of Ethiopia's peculiar feudal history, to impose socialism from above. But as the revolution institutionalizes and orders itself, there should be an expansion of social and political democracy, that is, the ability to permit the expression of differing values and needs *provided however that they accord with socialist values.* To put it differently, and taking the definition of freedom from the 1976 Cuban Constitution, 'The material conditions for its exercise [are] assuring its use to the exclusive service of the workers and of the interests of society' (Constitución de la Republica de Cuba, Art. 52). To extend democracy within such a frame ought clearly now to be considered. For if socialist democratic values and freedoms are not further extended, then Ethiopia may very well degenerate to the repressive political order found in Poland and other East European 'People's Republics' where power is often used against the interests of workers and society.

The creation of a party and the expansion of socialist democracy would go far in integrating Ethiopia firmly in the camp of true socialist-democratic states. And both actions would serve to secure and solidify the revolution.

Note. As this book went into print, Ethiopia announced on 10 September 1984 that a Workers' Party (WP) had been established. Mengistu was named the party's Secretary-General, while an eleven-member Politburo was chosen and a 136-member Central Committee was elected by COPWE delegates. The Dergue was apparently left standing. Seven members of the Politburo and 20 per cent of the Central Committee are of the military. The vanguard party's Politburo includes Mengistu, Fikre-Selassie Wogderess, Fisseha Desta, Tesfaye Gebre Kidan, Berhanu Bayih, Legesse Asfaw, Addis Tedlay, Hailu Yimenu, Amanuel Amde Michael, Shimelis Mazendia, and Alemu Abebe. Ethiopia's official designation was apparently altered to Ethiopian Socialist Democratic Republic. The creation of the WP suggests the elimination of COPWE and the completion of an important transitional phase of the revolution.

3 The Economy

Agriculture

In Ethiopia the economic system is dominated by the role of agriculture. With approximately 80 per cent of the population involved in agricultural pursuits and with 50 per cent of GDP originating from it, the position of agriculture within the economy is formidable (World Bank, 1983). As stated above, however, the emphasis on the political nature of the revolution, particularly within the context of land reform, has caused a certain amount of upheaval in economic productivity and planning. As with the Soviet Union

> the revolution from above that consolidated the socialist order in Russia and that marked the actual beginning of comprehensive socialist planning led to a sharp deterioration in the immediate economic situation, to a grievous disruption of the normal flow of agricultural production, and caused a painful drop in the standard of living. In this it was very much like most revolutionary breaks in history. [Baran, 1957, pp. 281-2.]

Despite the fact that the collectivization of land in Ethiopia was a vital step toward social and economic advancement in the long run, in the near term it caused a dramatic drop in agricultural production. For instance in 1977, two years after the implementation of the land reform programme, the volume of exports had dropped 34.7 per cent, while exports of coffee fell 13 per cent (IMF, December 1982, p. 187). Although in the proceeding years exports recovered somewhat, there is little doubt that the havoc brought about by the radical nature of the land reform programme greatly disrupted the agricultural economy (see Table 1).

Table 1. Volume of Exports(a) and Volume of Coffee Exports(b) (1975 = 100)

	1973	1974	1975	1976	1977	1978	1979	1980	1981
(a)	133.8	111.4	100	99.5	65.3	72	97.8	95.5	...
(b)	132	96	100	123	87	117	151	122	149

Source: Extracted from IMF Statistics, IMF, December, 1982, p. 187.

It is interesting to note that in terms of hides and skins, also afflicted by the land reform programme, exports took a similar turn (see Table 2).

Table 2. Volume of Exports of Hides and Skins (1975 = 100)

1973	1974	1975	1976	1977	1978	1979	1980	19-81
172	132	100	126	115	134	181	126	145

Source: Extracted from IMF Statistics, IMF, December 1982, p. 187.

Although it can be seen that coffee and skin exports have grown since the first economically destabilizing years of the revolution, the total volume of exports in 1980 was 4.5 per cent less than in 1975.

The problem surrounding exports, particularly as it affected the primary export, coffee, was made excruciatingly more difficult by the declining prices paid for export commodities. Whereas in 1978 the wholesale price of coffee was $1.55 per pound, in 1983 the price was approximately $1.25 and in 1984 $1.38 (IMF, April 1983, p. 58; Chicago Board of Trade, May 1983, September 1984). As a result, in 1981 (the latest total figures available) revenue from coffee exports was $227 million compared to $242.65 million in 1978 (IMF, ibid., p. 158). The decline in the price of skins was more precipitous. In 1979 the price quote on the Chicago Exchange was 73.02¢ per pound while in 1982 it was 39.90¢ (ibid., p. 58). Revenues in 1979 from the export of hides and skins brought in $68.26 million while in 1981 $47.54 million was collected (ibid., p. 158). Thus,

> Ethiopia's real GDP stagnated in 1981, following a growth of 3-4 per cent in 1980. Revenue from the principal export commodity, coffee, declined by 17 per cent, a 20 per cent volume increase being insufficient to match the fall in export prices. There was also a 10 per cent reduction in earnings from exports of hides and skins. . . . With other exports stagnating the total value of exports declined by 12 per cent [from] $425 million [in 1980]. [GATT, 1982, p. 157.]

The economic position of Ethiopia is even more forbidding if one compares present economic trends to the years prior to the revolution. Tables 1 and 2 indicate the marked decline in exports and production. The political factor that disturbed this agricultural sector of the economy was complicated by external economic forces beyond the control of Ethiopia. Both played a role in stymieing production, severely limiting the performance of agriculture.

Other than coffee the main agricultural crops are teff, a grain consumed in Ethiopia which forms about one-third of the cereal production and 'occupies [more than] half of the total area allotted to cereal production' (Bequele & Chole, 1969, p. 31), sorghum, barley, maize, wheat, the pulses which include chick peas, peas, broad beans, haricot beans and lentils and, finally, oilseeds. The declining state of production can be measured even more accurately when looking at the production of these goods. To indicate the extent of declining production, figures are given from 1970 to 1981 (see Table 3).

Table 3. Volume of Exports (in Millions of US $) of Pulses (a) and Oilseeds (b)

	1970	1971	1972	1973	1974	1975	1976	1977	1978	1979	1980	1981
(a)	7.6	18.7	12.6	37.3	49.2	31.3	27.0	21.0	8.3	10.8	11.8	12.0
(b)	13.7	15.5	23.5	25.1	46.3	40.5	15.0	8.4	5.9	4.5	7.4	7.2

Source: IMF, December 1982, p. 185.

The slumping productivity of pulses and oilseeds is quite extraordinary and indicates clearly that the volume production of the primary foodstuffs, both exported and consumed by Ethiopians, is close to disastrous. This is contrasted by the fact that in the 1970s it was assumed that productivity increase of these foods was 'promising' (Bequele & Chole, op. cit.). The pressure on the agricultural economy is further indicated by the overall trade balance (see Table 4).

Table 4. External Trade—in Millions of US$

	1978	1979	1980	1981
Imports	517	567	722	738
Exports	297	418	425	374
Balance	−220	−149	−297	−364

Source: IMF, April 1983, pp. 54, 55.

The collapse of world prices for agricultural commodities combined with reduced production has caused severe pressure on consumer prices. By 1982 consumer prices had risen 133.6 per cent from 1975, while from 1978 to 1982 the average yearly inflation rate was 15.32 per cent (IMF, April 1983, p. 158).

The increased cost of imported petroleum since the oil crisis of 1973 has affected Ethiopia as it has strained economies world-wide. In 1972 Ethiopia paid $17.25 million for imported oil; in contrast, in 1981 expenditure on oil was $171 million (IMF, April 1983, p. 158, and Dec. 1982, p. 185). Certainly, the problem was the price of oil rather than an increase in the amount purchased. Fuel imports in 1981 absorbed 46 per cent of export proceeds even though Ethiopia receives much of its oil from the Soviet Union at half the prices charged by the Organization of Petroleum Exporting Countries (OPEC) (*Ethiopia Profile*, December 1982, p. 9).

Thus, a number of factors came together during the height of the revolution to affect the agricultural economy of Ethiopia. There was the radical nature of the land reform programme that struck the economy negatively once the programme began to be implemented seriously. The tables above indicate that 1977 was the key year in that land reform implementation moved into high gear and production and exports were seriously affected. Although the indices begin to improve somewhat after that year *vis-à-vis* coffee, hides and skins, the same cannot be said for wheat, grain, the pulses and oilseeds: Ethiopia's primary indigenous foodstuffs. The economic indicators denote that the land reform programme, though politically valid and necessary, seriously handicapped the economy. Paul Baran's framework thus has application to Ethiopia. When a socialist revolution takes place there will almost certainly be a sharp economic constriction in the short term. Although Ethiopia, as indicated by the economic figures, is now beginning to recover from the economic after-effects of land reform, external factors continue to play a depressing economic role. The OPEC price of oil, though presently stabilized and lower than in 1981, is still 400 per cent higher than it was in 1972, while the world prices of agricultural commodities remain depressed as a result of the 1982-3 world recession. The Dergue/COPWE has no ability to shape these factors, and thus, to a large degree, the government is at the mercy of an economy shaped and influenced by world capitalism. The socialist states in the Eastern bloc, as well as the socialist governments of

France and Greece find themselves in the same position. The need and desire to stabilize the new economic order in Ethiopia is hampered by external economic factors that Ethiopia has no control over. Although the disincentives to agricultural production resulting from the old land tenure system have been removed by the Dergue's land reform programme, internal and external factors have combined to prevent economic and agricultural growth. Now, however, Dergue/COPWE no longer has to deal with the internal factor as land reform has stabilized. And with world commodity prices beginning to rise, the government is in a position to concentrate on the agricultural economy and ensure that it grows more rapidly than it has been able to since 1977.

One other element that is of concern regarding agriculture is the role of the USSR in providing economic aid to Ethiopia. Its role has essentially been limited to giving advice on the development of peasant associations and collective farms. Its aid in helping Ethiopia overcome its economic troubles is minimal (Ottaway, 1982, pp. 147–52). The poor performance of the Soviet economy (*1982* and *1983 Yearbook on International Communist Affairs*), the Soviet emphasis on military aid, and Soviet involvement in Afghanistan along with its heavy economic investment in Cuba and recently Poland, limit any economic role the Soviet Union might wish to play. So, despite the fact that Ethiopia has received extensive support in military equipment from the Soviet Union, economic aid is exceedingly small. Ethiopia's economic indebtedness to the Soviet Union in 1980 was only \$9.5 million compared to its economic debt to the United States of \$139 million in the same year (*Ten-Year Investment Programme*, 1981). Along the same lines the total flow of economic aid loan and grant capital from foreign sources into Ethiopia was only \$122 million in 1979 and \$243 million in 1980 (World Bank, 1981, p. 160; *Ten-Year Investment Programme*, 1981). Loans make up about 70 per cent and grants 30 per cent. Fifteen per cent of the monies however are normally earmarked for debt repayment for previous loans (ibid.). Such external assistance works out to \$7.5 per capita as compared to an average \$16.9 per capita for developing countries in general.

Although the Soviet Union is committed to continuing military aid to Ethiopia, preoccupation with other parts of the world together with emphasis on the military aspect, and internal and continuing economic problems, prevent it from giving any effective amount of economic aid.

As can be seen from the above figures only about 5.6 per cent of economic loans to Ethiopia in 1980 came from the Soviet Union. The German Democratic Republic and Cuba gave amounts totalling no more than $10 million in 1980, most of it coming from the East German government (*Ten-Year Investment Programme*). For 1983-6 the Soviet Union has approved loans and grants to Ethiopia totalling $384 million for economic development.

The overall picture is bleak indeed. The external debt amounted to $681 million in 1980 compared to $371 million in 1974/1975 (ibid.). Its national budget figures are no less discouraging (see Table 5).

Table 5. Revenue and Expenditures (Millions of US$)

	1976	1977	1978
Revenue	375.7	489.0	574.0
Expenditure	552.8	637.6	805.7
Deficit*	−177.1	−148.6	−231.7

Source: IMF, April 1983, p. 160.

*Excluding borrowing to finance the deficit, and excluding grants.

Ethiopia's Ten-Year Investment Programme, encompassing the decade 1980-90, attempts to come to grips with some of these issues. In so far as agriculture is concerned the plan sets out a strategy to 'increase the productivity of peasant agriculture through better production techniques, use of fertilizers, improved seeds . . . and by increasing farm labour productivity through cooperative ventures' (*Ten-Year Investment Programme*, 1981). It also opts for employing 'labour-intensive techniques of production in agriculture [and] rural road construction', the 'expansion of irrigated farming which would permit the realization of dependable and adequate food supplies and enhance the country's export capabilities', and 'raising the quality of livestock' for feed and export purposes (ibid.).

To this end the Programme sets out certain goals to be achieved by 1990: a GDP growth rate of 7.5 per cent, transformation of the economy where the industrial sector would grow from 16 per cent to 29 per cent and agriculture would shrink from 51 per cent to less than 35 per cent, increase domestic borrowing by increasing the savings rate from 6 per cent of GDP to 16 per cent, raise $8.2 thousand million through foreign loans and grants (ibid.).

The Programme becomes specific in targeting its objectives:

> (a) To lay down the material and technical bases for building socialism; (b) to achieve a structural transformation of the economy by increasing the proportion of industrial output with the aim of achieving self-sustained and self-reliant development; (c) to improve the cultural and material well-being of the people; (d) to conserve and develop the natural resources of the country; (e) to create job opportunities for gainful employment of the unemployed; (f) to distribute the benefits of production evenly in all regions of the country; (g) to build Ethiopia's foreign exchange capacity by producing for exports.
>
> The Program has the following targets: (a) double the gross domestic product in real terms by 1990; (b) provide employment for about 5 million people and reduce underemployment; (c) increase agricultural production by 60%; (d) increase industrial production four-fold; (e) increase the country's export revenue in real terms by 2.6 times; (f) provide basic health services to cover 85% of the rural population; (g) eradicate illiteracy and provide polytechnical education from grades 1 to 8 to children numbering 9 million; (h) construct 450,000 houses by 1990. [Ibid.]

The amount needed to finance the ten-year programme is $13.24 thousand million.

There can be no question that despite the depressed state of the economy the government is prepared to tackle the issue. Whether or not Ethiopia will be able to come up with the funding to finance the Programme, and even if it fails to meet many or all of its goals, socialist Ethiopia has indicated through its plan that it has the needs and interests of its peasants in mind. The Programme is noteworthy even if it fails: it signifies commitment to socialist values, and it points out that Dergue/COPWE is intent on trying to deal with the severe economic hardship caused by low productivity, high import costs, low prices for its exports, and minimal foreign economic aid. The state has moved, through this Programme, to try to cure its economic ills, but to do so within a socialist value system and a socialist framework. As Baran maintained, 'What is of crucial importance . . . is that the revolutionary turmoil during which a decline in output . . . and investment [occurs] is a transitory phenomenon. . . . Once the revolutionary crisis is over . . . and the new order politically and administratively stabilized, economic expansion' will take place (Baran, 1957, p. 265).

Through the Ten-Year Investment Programme Ethiopia is attempting to prod economic growth and development, increase the distribution of services to the peasants, and to thoroughly integrate the economy into the socialist political order. Ethiopia, in terms of Baran, is stabilized, and thus is both ready and prepared to wrestle with its economic problems. Although the Investment Programme deals with all sectors of the economy there is emphasis placed on agriculture, which clearly points to a recognition by the state that something drastic needs to be done to solve, or begin to solve, its economic problems.

It is vital that the apparent stress on the economy by the Investment Programme be followed through and given priority. A close look at the tables above indicates why this is necessary. In 1973 Ethiopia underwent a prolonged period of drought and famine that took the lives of hundreds of thousands of people. With the severe reduction of agricultural growth established by the figures stated above it is likely that another such tragedy might occur unless the Investment Programme is approached seriously. In early 1984 there were numerous reports that hunger was once again invading Ethiopia with a severity that approached that of 1973. It is therefore urgent that the government move rapidly to do what it can to increase agricultural production. The Investment Programme is an important, logical and necessary policy statement; but the policy must now be implemented. In 1984 production of cereals, grains and pulses was no more than in 1972, the year the Great Famine of 1973 had its origins, and the population in 1981 was 20 per cent larger than in 1972; it is clear that the situation is potentially devastating. With production remaining at almost historic lows in 1983 the government must move quickly to try to alleviate shortages. And although the state may not reach the goals it has set for itself in the Investment Programme (given economic conditions it may not), it must move to come as close as possible.

Ethiopia will have to increase the inflow of foreign exchange vastly in order to carry out the Investment Programme adequately. It will have to rely primarily on Western sources because of the Soviet bloc's reluctance, and inability, to provide effective economic aid. This will be discussed below, but it is questionable whether the capital needed for the Programme can be acquired. Also, Ethiopia's educational system, which is also analysed below within the context of state policies, is in extreme disrepair following the purges of students and faculty carried out through the previous ten years. Since that system would normally provide the expertise, at least to a large degree, to implement the plan, the question must be raised as to whether the present educational structure can provide the necessary skilled manpower. The assumption that it can is highly questionable. Although manpower is available that is politically and ideologically reliable, certain skills are necessary if the agricultural and technical targets of the Programme are to be met.

To a large degree the question of foreign exchange mirrors what happened in Ghana under Kwame Nkrumah between 1957 and 1966. Intent on creating a socialist state Ghana adopted the Programme of the Convention People's Party for Work and Happiness in April 1962. It opted for the adoption of socialism that was predicated on attracting a huge amount of foreign capital from Western sources. It was apparently a necessary contradiction so that agriculture and manufactures could be developed to support economically Nkrumah's style of socialism. But as the price of cocoa continued to decline agricultural development was stymied, the Work and Happiness Programme faltered, and in 1966 Nkrumah was overthrown in a military coup (see Fitch & Oppenheimer, 1966). Ethiopia must be careful not to fall into the same contradiction. Although foreign exchange is vital to the Ten-Year Investment Programme, Ethiopia must try to get its revenue from sources more neutral to socialism than the British were to Nkrumah's ideology. Great Britain, although advancing credits, was unhappy with Nkrumah in the final analysis and refused to continue the support necessary for Ghanaian socialism to work (ibid.). As Fitch and Oppenheimer maintained

> the problem of economic growth is not solved . . . by stimulating growth within the old economic structures and by intensifying the existing relationships. Growth can only be attained by smashing the old structures and severing the old relationships. Only then is it possible to achieve rational, democratic, collective control over economic inputs and outputs—that is, socialist planning. [Ibid., pp. 81-2.]

Clearly, Ethiopia's Programme is more purely socialist than Ghana's plan was. Ethiopia has altered the old economic relationships, and continues on that course. If the sources of foreign exchange accept Ethiopia's basic framework, then it is possible that Ethiopia can attain the wherewithal to support its ten-year plan. Although other variables enter into the equation, such as education, skilled labour, and a pool of motivated workers who will be the cutting edge of the plan, a major problem will have been successfully dealt with: attaining Western foreign capital for

the purpose of radically advancing the economy, particularly the agricultural sector, of a genuine socialist state.

Judging from its investment plan Ethiopia has come to grips with its agricultural needs. At the same time its leadership has served notice that the economy must be coordinated politically and ideologically with socialism. Theoretically and technically the Investment Programme is a sound policy statement. Whether Ethiopia will be able to meet the goals it has set for itself within the Investment Programme is a question that for the moment can not be answered. If the foreign aid is forthcoming, and if the manpower necessary for the Programme's implementation is there then the policy statement may become at least a partial reality. Important too however is stabilization of coffee prices, and increased production of agricultural products. In essence, external and internal factors must both be favourable if the Ten-Year Investment Programme is to have any chance of success. But, Dergue/COPWE has moved to confront the agricultural problems, and has done so in such a way that socialism can be advanced in the process. This is an important ideological condition. It signifies collaboration between the economy and the polity that portends an integrated social revolution rather than one that is inherently antagonistic.

Manufactures

In 1967 Ethiopia expended only 2 per cent of its government expenditures on agriculture; the land reform programme of socialist Ethiopia and the Ten-Year Investment Programme expands the allocation of money for agriculture extensively (Bequele & Chole, 1969, p. 48). As far as the manufacturing industry is concerned Ethiopia plans to increase its spending similarly.

Manufacturing is dominated by food, textile and beverage products. But domination is a misleading term as in 1965 'there were only 24[illegible] establishments in manufacturing industry in the whole of Ethiopia, with nearly half of them situated in Addis Ababa' (ibid., p. 52). And, in the same year only 43,583 people were employed in that sector of the economy (ibid., p. 54). By 1980, only 7 per cent of the labour force was employed in industry (World Bank, 1983). Exports of food, textile and beverage products is minimal, constituting somewhat more than 5 per cent of total export trade, with food the dominant manufacturing export commodity (IMF, December 1982, pp. 54, 66–7). Overall, food makes up about 19 per cent of investment in manufacturing; beverages and bottling—8 per cent; textiles—29 per cent; building—12 per cent; the chemical industry—19 per cent; with tobacco, leather and shoes, wood, printing, steel, cement and others making up the balance (*Ethiopia Statistical Abstract*, 1970–3, 'Industry'). Only 16 per cent of GDP originates from manufacturing and industry (World Bank, 1983).

The Ten-Year Investment Programme envisages a radical restructuring of Ethiopia's manufacturing base. Of the $13.24 thousand million planned to support the Programme, 15 per cent would be allocated to manufacturing, as compared to 20 per cent for agriculture. An additional 18 per cent would be invested in mining, energy, water, and construction, while 26 per cent would be given over to transport and communication, and 15 per cent to social services (*Ten-Year Investment Programme*, 1981). It is clear that the state views the Programme as enabling Ethiopia to expand its manufacturing sector dramatically.

There are however significant problems that provoke doubt as to whether expansion on the scale envisioned by the state is possible. Agriculture would play an almost monopolistic role in terms of development due to its overwhelming position in the economy; the need to continue to maintain a large military force in the Ogaden and in Eritrea absorbs capital and human resources that could otherwise be used for industrial and agrarian growth; if the total funds necessary for the success of the Programme are not attained it is more than likely that the manufacturing sector will suffer first from a cut in funding; and finally, 'the practicability of such a programme depends . . . on the availability of resources for a significant expansion of industry, in other words, on the capacity of agriculture to provide a surplus large enough to support a sufficient volume of industrial construction' (Baran, 1957, p. 277). Due to the questionable assumption that Ethiopia will acquire the outside funding it is counting on for the completion of the Programme, the last variable comes directly into play, thus suggesting an alternative manufacturing policy.

Ethiopia ought to concentrate on developing small-scale industry for import substitution, to reduce, albeit to a limited extent, its balance of payments deficit, and to increase employment realistically, i.e., employment in the manufacturing sector is very tiny and it is unlikely that a major expansion of employment can take place since the manufacturing base is not there to absorb unrealistic expansion. That capacity does not exist. Ethiopia, in terms of the market, has not changed much since 1969 when Assefa Bequele and Eshetu Chole argued that

> Industrial development in Ethiopia is low. . . . The most significant [reason] the narrowness of the market. Over 90 per cent of the Ethiopian population is in the subsistence sector and . . . out of consideration for purposes of major cash transactions. . . . The narrowness of the internal market is . . . matched by the narrowness of the international market for Ethiopian manufactured products. [pp. 57–8.]

Despite the fact that monies are also allocated for development of roads and a transportation grid, at the moment internal transportation is so poor that most people do not live near a main arterial road. This is a major handicap to the development of industry on the scale that Ethiopia plans.

It would appear then that there should first of all be concentration on a major expansion of the agricultural economy, with a concurrent effort at supporting the growth of small scale and handicraft type manufactures. Once a large enough agricultural surplus coupled with a stabilization of world prices occurs, then a significant expansion of industry should be considered. Otherwise, as Baran maintains, a manufactures programme will not be practical, and will not lead to a smashing of the old economic dependency. This is precisely the dilemma that Nkrumah found himself in, and it is one the leaders of Ethiopia should at all cost try to avoid. The theory of dependency is very real, as Andre Gunder Frank has indicated (1981) and the policy presently advocated by the Programme would only increase Ethiopia's dependency on the West. If, however, agriculture and a growing internal market could support the primary elements of the Programme, there would be less reliance on the Western states that historically have prohibited, or helped to prohibit, Ethiopia's economic growth.

Mining is currently an insignificant element of the national economy, with little likelihood that it can develop in the near future. Gold, manganese ore and platinum exist but capital and the necessary infrastructure for extraction remains unavailable. From 1980 to February 1983 Ethiopia's gold reserves have remained stable indicating little mining activity (IMF, April 1983, pp. 158–9). Less mining of Ethiopia's other minerals occurs. Although extraction of its gold deposits would be of great help to Ethiopia's liquidity position, and despite the fact that mining is considered in the Investment Programme, the talent and capital necessary will not become available concurrently and thus it is more than unlikely that mining will move dramatically upwards from its minor position in the economy. In the area of mining particularly Ethiopia can expect little economic help from the Soviet Union. 'The USSR is the world's second largest producer of gold (an estimated 346 tonnes were extracted in 1981), and sales of this precious metal provide it with a source of funds apparently more residual than planned in the five-year context' (NATO, 8 April 1983, p. 2). The Soviet Union is unlikely to aid Ethiopia extensively in developing a gold industry that would compete with its own trade. Some efforts are being made however as the USSR supplied $6 million in 1984 to increase extraction at the Adola gold mine.

The Politics of Economic Growth

In terms of pure economics Ethiopia is affected by limited agricultural growth, a manufacturing sector that is virtually insignificant, and external factors that serve to inhibit the development of both. At the same time Ethiopia has taken advanced political decisions affecting its economy. It has moved to develop a political economy through the Ten-Year Investment Programme. By moving in this direction Ethiopia has indicated that political factors weigh as heavily as do those purely economic elements. Although this may inhibit economic growth, in that foreign funding may not be so forthcoming, it can, in the long run, serve to develop economic growth by relating the economy to socialist planning and moving to break the traditional economic relationship with the West. For although Western capital will be required to support the Investment Programme, the economic framework established in the plan is clearly socialist. Ethiopia, like all socialist countries, is interested in maintaining trading relations with capitalist and socialist nations alike, but to do so within a framework that advances socialism, rather than capitalism. Its desire is to contribute to the emergence 'of a society in which development will supplant stagnation, . . . growth will take the place of decay' (Baran, 1957, p. 300). Whatever deficiencies exist within the Ten-Year Investment Programme, there can be no question but that the plan is the first coherent economic policy statement ever to evolve from any Ethiopian government. That in itself is historically noteworthy. But, the Programme is more than historically important. It lays the foundation for the emergence of a fully integrated socialist economy. And though elements of the Programme may fail to reach the stated goals, and though some parts of the Programme may be too far-reaching and thus may not work, the policy moves Ethiopia firmly into doctrinaire and fairly orthodox socialist economics. Ethiopia, in terms of economic theory, has travelled an extraordinary distance since the 1974 revolution. Hopefully the policy goals can be met; but even if they cannot Ethiopia has let it be known that a socialist political economy is now the theoretical construct of the state. The investment policy statement has institutionalized a new economic order that, finally, concerns itself with the betterment of the masses. In economic terms, as well as politically, the Investment Programme serves as confirmation that the original promises of the revolution are being kept.

4 The Regime's Policies

Domestic Policies

Since the revolution radical and positive changes have taken place in the education and health sectors. Just as land reform had beneficial consequences for the rural population, so too did changes in health and education benefit that group of people who were neglected for centuries. On the other hand, with the revolution came changes in religious policy that have not always found support among the populace. Bound by a fierce traditional loyalty to either Islam or the Ethiopian Orthodox Church, the state found it difficult to socialize the people to accept the policy of allowing all religions equal participation. At the same time, Dergue/COPWE punished opposition by the churches in much the same way it dealt with opposition from other sectors of society–violently–and this also caused severe strains within that stratum of the population whose religious affiliation was vibrant. Still, since health and education, in concert with land reform, affected more people directly in their daily lives than did religion, the programmes advocated by socialist Ethiopia in these areas were welcomed and added to the growing support to Dergue/COPWE by Ethiopians. The policies further institutionalized and strengthened the relationship between people and state.

Education

In Ethiopia the educational system has been too small and neglected, and has traditionally served the urban population. During the 1960s the country had one of the lowest literacy rates in Africa: '5-6 per cent of the population over 10 years of age were literate; by 1970 this had risen to 9-10 per cent' (*Syncrisis*, 1974, p. 4). The US Department of Health, Education and Welfare estimated that in 1969 17 per cent of males ten years of age or older were literate compared to 2 per cent of females (ibid.). The correlation between literacy and urban areas, and illiteracy and rural areas is clear. In 1969 Ethiopia reported 'that about 37 per cent of the urban population 10 years of age or older were literate, versus 3.5 per cent of the rural population' (ibid.). The urban/rural dichotomy is reaffirmed by figures on school attendance. 'With regard to school attendance, we found that in 1964–5 about 69% of all young people between the ages of 7 and 14 living in urban centers were in school. This was true of only 3.1 per cent of rural children in the same age group' (Ginsberg & Smith, 1967, p. 32). But, even these figures are deceiving. In 1966–7 409,710 students were enrolled in elementary school, 36,480 in junior secondary school, and 23,832 in senior secondary school; from 1961 to 1966, 74.3 per cent of all students left school between the first and sixth grade, while 72.5 per cent of the balance dropped out between the seventh and twelfth grade (*School Census for Ethiopia*, 1967, pp. 6, 8). In 1971 about 3.1 per cent of the total population were enrolled in schools, but the regions of Shoa and Eritrea had the highest concentration of student enrolments; this is not surprising since Ethiopia's two major urban centres, Addis Ababa and Asmara, are located there.

In addition facilities were inadequate and deficiencies in teacher qualification existed. In the years just prior to the revolution there were only 2,518 schools with merely 16,024 classrooms (*Syncrisis*, op. cit., p. 4). With teaching being a low status occupation, as well as a low paid profession, 'teaching is not regarded as an attractive long-term career by the educated and few want to teach in rural areas' (ibid.). Many who failed to qualify for senior secondary school entered the primary teaching field. Only two universities exist: Addis Ababa University, with about 3,000 enrolled students, and the University of Asmara. In 1965–6 the educational system was served by only 11,501 teachers at all levels of education (Bequele & Chole, 1969, p. 105).

It is starkly evident that the conspicuous features of education in Ethiopia prior to the revolution added up to an extremely low level of investment in human resources. Its small size and urban emphasis, low quality and scarcity of teachers, an imbalance between regions, and an imbalance between the sexes created a situation where education existed in name only. Even though in 1966–7 the Ministry of Education was allocated the second largest proportion of government funds ($46.2 million) (*Ethiopia Statistical Abstract*, 1966, p. 149), the impact of these funds on the educational system was insignificant.

The present government has made a concerted effort to develop its human resources through education. In its Ten-Year Investment Programme it plans to eradicate illiteracy and enrol 9 million students through the eighth grade by 1990. But, in the short term it has also done much. A massive literacy campaign was launched in 1979 that emphasizes the rural areas. Using China's barefoot-doctor model Ethiopia has sponsored locally, or sent into the interior thousands of semi-educated 'teachers' whose sole purpose is to teach writing and reading within the context of the peasant associations and the kebelles. "'I used to think that reading and writing were something magic, something for people of high birth," Tiruwork Yilma told me. A woman of 50, she was experiencing her first exposure to education. "Now I can sign my own name instead of using my thumbprint, and I can read the numbers on the bus. I feel part of a larger world"' (Caputo, 1983, p. 623). It has been estimated by one source that between 1974 and 1983 the literacy level in Ethiopia has been raised from 10 per cent to 35 per cent (ibid.). Though clearly a generous estimate there is little doubt that literacy rates have been raised substantially, and are presently at the probable level of about 17 per cent. The literacy classes and their impact are best summed up in the words of an Oromo farmer. 'Life is much better here now. . . . I go to literacy class for two hours every morning. I can read a little and am learning to write. It may not do much for me—I am old. But my children, they can already read and write. They will have a better life' (ibid., p. 625).

But there is also emphasis on the traditional educational sector. More schools are being constructed and students are being increased. In Bale region, for instance, where thirty-two elementary and one secondary school existed before 1974 there are now 186 elementary, fifteen junior secondary and three senior secondary schools (ibid.).

By recognizing the importance of education for its own sake Dergue/COPWE has permitted education to become a political weapon in its struggle to tie the population to its policies. In meeting a long-standing need and desire, and by allowing the peasants to see a better future for their children through education, the state has moved decisively. And in so doing, it further embraces the rural population and remains consistent in fulfilling the expectations created by the revolution. By increasing expenditure in the traditional sectors of the educational system (even though in the 1970s it purged its student body), as well as developing the barefoot teacher campaign, the state has begun to move strongly towards bettering the everyday lives of its citizens. And it is doing so within a socialist framework: without regard to class or status, sex, age, rural or urban considerations. It is education based on need and equality.

Health

Health care under the regime of Haile Selassie was also neglected. Tuberculosis was, and remains, widespread and affects 30-40 per cent of the population (*Syncrisis*, op. cit., p. 14). Malaria is endemic. In 1958 there was an epidemic that took the lives of more than 150,000 people. Intestinal parasites affect the lives of millions and this is considered second in importance only to malaria (ibid., p. 16). Leprosy is also widespread and it is assumed that 10 per cent of the population will contract the disease at some point in their lives.

Nutrition is substandard with 'an average caloric deficit of up to 400 calories per person per day' (ibid., p. 19). This is exacerbated by the fact that the many rivers and waterways are often a primary focus for the dissemination of human schistosomiasis. In addition, in 1974 it was estimated that 75 per cent of the adult population has or has had venereal disease.

The infrastructure of health care was miserable. In 1974 there were only 8,415 hospital beds in eighty-five hospitals serving the entire country (ibid., p. 26). Most of the hospitals were in urban centres. Local health care centres, the primary medical structure available in the interior, in the same year numbered only ninety-three! In Bale, for instance, only two health care centres were in existence prior to the revolution. In 1972 only 347 doctors existed with the overall doctor/population ratio being one per 68,983, 'one of the lowest in the world' (ibid., p. 27). It was in Addis Ababa, however, that 45 per cent of the physicians practised. In a classic diplomatic understatement the US Department of Health, Education and Welfare stated in 1974 that 'the health status of the population is poor' (ibid., p. v). By 1980, the doctor/population ratio *improved* slightly to one per 58,490 (World Bank, 1983).

Although Ethiopia eventually hopes to provide health care centres to cover 85 per cent of the rural population, it has already created hundreds of health stations throughout the country to provide minimal health care and, perhaps even more important, to provide education in health care. These centres, among other things, teach mothers simple techniques for diagnosing and treating common ailments affecting children, dispense pills for aiding in the treatment of minor ailments, utilize scales so people can use the fact and concept of weight to discern medical problems. The government sends to these stations poorly trained medical teams, again on the order of the barefoot doctor, to provide medical support to rural peoples. These health stations, like their educational counterpart, are set up within peasant associations and kebelles. They also serve to deal with the problems of drought and famine. Maize, flour and butter are presently being distributed through the health stations because of drought and to prevent a repetition of the 1973–4 disaster. Clearly, Ethiopia is presently trying to do what it can to begin to deal with the severe health problems that continue to afflict the country.

Poor health and education are part of the common heritage the socialist government has to contend with. Both were so neglected during the pre-revolutionary period that the present government faces an almost insurmountable task. With limited capital available to it, and with myriad other issues to contend with, the state is doing what it can. Though it is not enough, it is clearly perceived by the population as being helpful. Having never received any social or economic largess in the past, the present rural education and health facilities are serving an important social and political role. They indicate to the peasant that the state is trying to do what it can and is attempting to fulfil its revolutionary promises; at the same time since the peasant is obviously responding so favourably it secures the relationship between peasant and socialist Ethiopia. Together with the land reform programme, and the attempt to create greater equity within the area of urban housing, Dergue/COPWE has made great political strides in developing its connection to the people. Whether its Ten-Year Investment Programme can alleviate the health and education problems in the long run is yet to be seen. But, strides have been made and a concerted effort has begun to deal, finally, with these issues. The government has shown that it has the will; it lacks the capital and skilled manpower to fully confront the issues. But it has begun.

Improving and developing primary health care and educational facilities on the local level can act as a stimulus to economic and political development. Economic and political organizations can be strengthened through the training of local populations. In addition the primary component of ensuring a causal relationship between primary health care and political development is making the population aware of the benefits available to it in the short run. The people will see that in addition to an immediate resolution to their physical problems, they can ensure a better and more fruitful life for themselves in the long run. Ethiopia's local educational and health programmes are truly political development programmes. For political and economic consciousness is being raised and political perceptions are being altered. Ethiopia's investment in human capital is more than a collection of projects; it is part of a process that draws a relationship between health and education to politics and ties the national entity closer to the countryside. As Mao often put it, the people are changing their subjective cognition and are advancing from one stage of political development to another.

Religion

The effect of religion on Ethiopians has been enormous. For the Ethiopian Orthodox Christian life is merely a bridge to the other world. The saying 'Man proposes but God disposes' has deeply penetrated the ontology of the Ethiopian peasant. Expecting little in this life has created a fatalism and resignation that to a large degree allowed Ethiopians to be oppressed for centuries. The role of religion and tradition has not served Ethiopian peasants well but their effects have been overwhelming and longlasting.

In Islam too, God rather than the state predominates. The purpose of the state in Islam is to enforce the principles of the Shariah, the laws derived from the Koran, the Sunna–the Hadith and decisions of Muhammad, Ijma' and Ijtihad. Under Islam, sovereignty belongs to God alone, with both rulers and ruled working for the glory of God whose wishes and commands must be followed if happiness here and in the hereafter is to be achieved.

With upwards of 80 per cent of Ethiopians adhering to either Islam or Ethiopian Orthodoxy the power of both churches was prodigious and of real consequence to the everyday lives of the people.

The revolution however brought real and lasting change in religious policy. Immediately upon the removal of Haile Selassie the Dergue declared that the Ethiopian Orthodox Church would no longer exist as the official church of the state. The position of Islam was upgraded so that higher officials appeared together with Coptic officials at state functions. All religions however were officially recognized as having equal status before the eyes of the state. In 1977 however the Dergue moved against the Ethiopian Orthodox Church indicating that it was no longer treating religion as a neutral political entity. On 18 February the patriarch of the Ethiopian Orthodox Church, Abuna Theophilos, was removed from office and arrested. He was accused by the Dergue of crimes against the Ethiopian people, including the accumulation of millions of dollars. This was followed by an attack on all religions in an attempt to limit the false consciousness that so enveloped the masses. Clearly, after 1977 the Dergue felt in a position strong enough to take on the religious sector of society. Between 1977 and 1982 a number of Coptic church leaders disappeared, while others have been assassinated (*Ethiopia Profile*, February 1982, p. 6). In late 1981 Ethiopian Archbishop Mathias fled Ethiopia and received asylum in Great Britain. In Eritrea and Tigre the Islamic church has had its activities sharply curtailed by the government due to the war against the secessionist rebels. Thus both the Ethiopian Orthodox Church and Islam have had their power and influence reduced.

In early 1982 Sweden and Norway maintained that the Ethiopian Evangelical Church had been seized by the government and that the 600 Lutheran churches had been closed. At about the same time the Canadian Association for Ethiopian Jews, and the Los Angeles-based Simon Wiesenthal Center accused Ethiopia of arresting and torturing Ethiopian Jews (Falashas), and of engaging in a general campaign of anti-semitism. Earlier, in August 1981, Rev. John Gatu, chairman of the All-Africa Conference of Churches had criticized Ethiopia's persecution of religious leaders.

It is apparent that Ethiopia has embarked on a new policy *vis-à-vis* religion. While at first merely limiting the role of the Ethiopian Orthodox Church, the new policy entails a broad attack on the role and authority of all religious forces. While it can be maintained, and is by some, that the policy is perhaps anti-semitic or anti-Catholic, it is probably more accurate to see in this attack a continuation of the Dergue's policy of sweeping aside all countervailing political forces. Religion is clearly viewed by Ethiopian leaders as a political power, and thus its authority must be curtailed, and possibly eliminated. This is clearly the thrust of the policy that originated in 1977 when the Abuna was arrested.

But Dergue/COPWE has been clever in its carrying out of this policy. It has not allowed a vacuum. The various programmes and policies that were established by the state have shown the Ethiopian peasant, and in fact the entire population, that the authority of the church would be replaced by a state authority sensitive to their needs and desires. Although the destabilization of church authority has been protested both inside and outside Ethiopia, the government refused to back down and whatever internal unrest existed has been generally pacified. As with the revolution itself it has been remarkable how quickly the population as a whole has come to accept the radical changes that have taken place.

In its religious policy Dergue/COPWE has moved toward Marxist orthodoxy. And although Ethiopia is often condemned for advancing to such an orthodox position (see Rapoport, 1979), there can be little doubt that such a policy is congruent with Ethiopia's ideology. Sooner or later the position of all the churches had to be attacked if their countervailing authority, that was in direct contradistinction to the new Ethiopia, was to be destroyed.

In the area of domestic policies the state has been consistent to its ideology and practice. It has moved to create new and innovative programmes in the areas of housing, health, education and rural land, while at the same time it has struck hard at structures and authorities that inherently oppose the new socialist order. From the beginning, the new Ethiopian leadership has stuck to a consistent line and it has hardly deviated from that position. The lives of Ethiopia's poorest citizens have been improved, while those whose status and class was once superior have been levelled. It is an approach that has been uniformly applied to all sectors and peoples of Ethiopia.

Ethiopia's tendency to emphasize its economic and social responsibilities, and to place political needs within an economic and social context fits into the framework of human rights as culturally and traditionally stressed in the Third World. In underscoring this perspective Ethiopia gives 'credence to the notion of human dignity as consisting of economic rights rather than [predominantly] political or civil rights. Freedom from starvation, the right for all to enjoy the . . . benefits of a developed economy, and freedom from exploitation became the articulated goals of many Third World countries' (Pollis & Schwab, 1980, p. 9). The Western conception of human rights, based on the conceptualization of natural right and natural law is rejected as inapplicable since it is contrary to the cultural, ideological and traditional values inherent in Third World societies (ibid., ch. 1).

From both a non-Western and a socialist perspective, Ethiopia has taken a correct ideological position in its domestic policies. The entire range of its economic and social policies contain within their frame the politics of equity. Political rights and economic and social rights have a common core and cannot be separated one from the other.

Foreign Policy

Virtually since the first days of the revolution Ethiopia has had to contend with foreign policy issues that tested the very ability of the regime's survival. Confronted with a secessionist war in Eritrea under way since 1962 and an attack by Somalia in the Ogaden, Ethiopia has had to struggle militarily to ensure the durability of the revolution. Concurrently the new socialist government severed its relationship with the United States, which was long-standing and traditional, and fashioned a military connection with the Soviet Union. All this political/military activity led to a certain amount of instability and turmoil that, in hindsight, forced the Ethiopian leadership to clarify its nationalist/internationalist position and its socialist ideology more rapidly than if conditions had been calm.

The Horn of Africa, comprising Ethiopia, Somalia and Djibouti, is an area of the world whose strategic location has thrust it into the international arena as a potential crisis zone. Overlapping the Middle East and the Indian Ocean, it flanks the oil-rich states of Arabia, controls the Bab el Mandeb Straits, which in turn is one of the narrow arteries of Israel's lifeline, dominates a part of the Gulf of Aden and Indian Ocean through which oil tankers are constantly moving, and overlooks the passages where the Red Sea, the Gulf of Aden, and the Indian Ocean converge.

> Geography is undoubtedly the force that has evoked superpower concern with the Horn of Africa, as the contending interests of the Soviet Union and the United States converge at this point around both the Middle East and oil diplomacy. . . . The Horn's proximity to the Middle East and its significance as regards the worldwide defence strategy of both superpowers places it in the position of being caught up in the strategic military and political policies of both the Soviet Union and the United States [Schwab, 1978, p. 9].

United States' strategy as applied to the Horn of Africa and the Indian Ocean was clarified by Admiral Stansfield Turner, former Director of the Central Intelligence Agency, and by former Defense Secretary James R. Schlesinger,

> The fundamental role of our Navy has been sea control . . . There are fundamentally two threats that the presence of a naval force can imply: to do harm to a nation by projecting power directly onto its territory or to sever a nation's sea lines of communication through blockade or sea denial. [Turner, 1977, pp. 342-3.]
>
> The Soviet Union has become a major sea power only in the last decade. . . . The level of US presence in the Indian Ocean has been prudent. . . . In a period of historical transition toward a new set of power relations, only the United States among the Western nations has the stature to ensure that the balance is maintained. [Schlesinger, 1975.]

For the Soviet Union the situation was similar. Due to Soviet perceptions of its own weakness during the 1962 Cuban missile crisis 'the Soviet Navy's role was no longer defined [solely] to defence of the Soviet Union's coast, but became long range' (Edmonds, 1975, p. 42). Thus, Ethiopia in its foreign affairs had to contend with the national interests of both superpowers while at the same time ensuring that its own national and international interests would be met. Tension with both superpowers was therefore very likely.

While Schlesinger and Turner served under Presidents Gerald Ford and Jimmy Carter respectively, US policy towards the Horn of Africa has only hardened in the 1980s under President Ronald Reagan.

> Reagan . . . has concentrated more singlemindedly on resisting 'Soviet adventurism' in Africa. . . . [One major area] on which United States policy should focus: the Horn. . . . The Reagan administration states clearly that it will not remain on the sidelines, allowing its Soviet adversary to probe with a free hand. Rather, it asserts its intentions to counter Soviet [and Cuban] involvement with American involvement. [Rothchild & Ravenhill, 1983, pp. 346, 348, 349.]

War with Somalia and the Development of Socialist Alliances

In mid-July 1977 the Western Somali Liberation Front (WSLF), with military aid and support troops from Somalia, stormed the Ogaden and captured 90 per cent of it. At this time Somalia, under socialist rule, was supported by the Soviet Union, and Ethiopia, which had broken with the United States in 1977, was helpless. The Soviet Union, however, feeling closer ideologically to Ethiopia and recognizing Ethiopia as the key actor in the vital region of the Horn, particularly with its Red Sea ports in Eritrea, agreed to supply Ethiopia with the military weaponry to defend itself. The Soviet Union 'hoped to bridge the Somalia-Ethiopia dispute through common ideology, and at the same time it believed that it could maintain an interest in both countries' (Schwab, 1981, p. 311). In November however, Somalia expelled all Soviet advisers and closed the Soviet naval facilities in Berbera, overlooking the Gulf of Aden. As a result the Soviet Union tied itself more closely to Ethiopia. An extensive airlift of Soviet weapons—to the value of $875 million—allowed Ethiopia, in March 1978, thoroughly to defeat and expel the Somalis. Cuba, which sent more than 16,000 military troops and advisers to Ethiopia to participate in the battle for the Ogaden, and the Soviet Union, which sent 1,500 military advisers, secured a close and binding relationship with Ethiopia by helping it in its hour of need. The German Democratic Republic and the People's Democratic Republic of Yemen also supported Ethiopia by sending military and technical advisers.

Somalia, in its outrageous attempt to take advantage of the internal disorders in Ethiopia during the violent year of 1977, actually forced the Soviet Union to rethink its policy on the Horn more quickly than it might otherwise have. Ethiopia, pushed to the wall by the Somali invasion moved rapidly into the socialist military orbit recognizing that ideologically the Soviet Union was its natural ally, and that militarily it had no choice but to establish that alliance immediately. Soviet and Ethiopian interests converged. Ethiopia needed the Soviets to stave off Somalia's attempt to reclaim what it maintained was its 'lost territory', while the Soviet Union secured a major ideological ally, and would be able to eventually attain 'a valuable prize . . . a coastal region, which helps explain the Soviet reversal' (Selassie, 1980, p. 131).

> In 1962 the Soviets gambled in Cuba and lost. This time [in the Ogaden] they may not lose. They have port facilities in Aden allowing them to continue to dominate the southern end of the Red Sea and the Gulf of Aden and they could retain access to Ethiopian ports [in Eritrea]. Successful implementation of this policy would give the Soviets absolute dominance in the Red Sea, control over the Gulf of Aden and the entrance to the Indian Ocean, quick access to the Persian Gulf. It would also ensure the Soviet Union an overriding position as against the United States on the Horn of Africa. [Schwab, 1978, p. 18.]

After the successful conclusion of the war the Soviet Union moved rapidly to secure its relationship with Ethiopia, ensuring that it would remain within the socialist orbit, and also moved to attain access to the Red Sea. In November 1978 Ethiopia signed a twenty-year Treaty of Friendship and Cooperation with the Soviet Union, and a similar treaty with the German Democratic Republic was concluded a year later. To improve Ethiopia's military position, between 1977 and 1983, the Soviets supplied Ethiopia with over $2 thousand million in military aid, and through 1984 the figure is closer to $3 thousand million. Despite the fact that Ottaway maintains that the Soviets have not developed any major influence over Ethiopia (1982, p. 149), the Soviet Navy in 1981 developed an anchorage in the Dahlak Islands off Ethiopia on the Red Sea, and was in 1983 reported to be in the process of constructing a naval base there (*1982 Yearbook on International Communist Affairs*, p. 17). Also, the Soviet Navy has access to the port facilities at Massawa and Assab. And although it is true that the Ethiopian government is refusing to allow the Soviets to construct naval facilities there, there can be no question but that the Soviet aid to Ethiopia, initiated at the time of the Somalia war, has given them influence and access over the Red Sea and the Indian Ocean.

The states of the socialist commonwealth have increased their relationship with Ethiopia since the 1970s. In 1981 Bulgaria and Ethiopia concluded a Treaty of Friendship, Cooperation and Consular Convention. And in 1982 Ethiopia attended the Fifth Congress of the Communist Party of Vietnam, signed a protocol agreement strengthening cultural and scientific cooperation with the Soviet Union, and concluded an agreement with the German Democratic Republic that recognized their common responsibility to a 'Marxist-Leninist party in socialist construction'.

Ethiopia, along with two other pro-Soviet states, Libya and South Yemen, signed a Treaty of Friendship and Cooperation in 1981. President Ali Nasir Muhammad al-Hassani of South Yemen stated that the group would be a 'material force taking action on the path of joint struggle against all forms of conspiracy and aggression [from imperialist forces] which threaten the peoples of these three countries' (ibid.). In the same year Ethiopia and Cuba signed a series of scientific, cultural, agricultural, educational, health and joint-construction agreements. Cuba, which still has over 3,000 troops stationed in Ethiopia, continues to aid Ethiopia both militarily and economically.

The alliances with the socialist commonwealth remain important for more than ideological reasons. Periodically fighting still occurs in the Ogaden, and the remaining Cuban troops and Soviet aid remain vital. In July 1982, 7,000 Ethiopian troops, in support of the Somali Democratic Salvation Front (SDSF), invaded and occupied two Somali villages along the border east of the Ogaden. The Ethiopian air force bombed Somali troop positions in the frontier villages. The Ethiopian attack was in response to continued Somali support for the WSLF's attempt to wrest the Ogaden from Ethiopia. While the siege was eventually lifted this type of sporadic military activity can be expected to continue.

The United States however, has responded politically, diplomatically and militarily to the events in the Horn. In 1981 the United States delivered $40 million in 'defensive' military aid to Somalia. The US State Department announced that this aid 'is part of a strategic framework in response to the Soviet threat in the region'. The United States also developed plans in 1981 to have a string of military bases in the Red Sea, the Horn of Africa, and the Indian Ocean by 1986 at a cost of more than $2 thousand million. As part of a comprehensive strategy for dealing with the growth of Soviet power in the region, naval bases are planned for development in Egypt, Somalia, Kenya and Oman, while the United States' naval position on the island of Diego Garcia is to be strengthened. By 1983, $24 million was sent to Somalia to repair facilities in the port of Berbera, while $26 million was allocated to dredge the Kenyan port of Mombasa. Between 1980 and 1983 the United States sent Somalia $85 million in military and financial assistance (*New York Times*, 22 April 1983), and to Oman $165 million in military aid (*New York Times*, 6 April 1983). The United States has also expanded its aid programme to the Sudan, which, in conjunction with Egypt, views itself as a bulwark against Libya and Ethiopia, and has developed its relationship with Saudi Arabia, Kuwait and North Yemen. 'The United States . . . has . . . increased its military and political influence [in these countries] in an attempt to match Soviet influence in Ethiopia, South Yemen, Libya, and on the Indian Ocean. . . . The Horn of Africa and the states that surround it have thus been pushed into the centre of the cold war' (Schwab, 1978, p. 20).

Somalia's invasion of the Ogaden was the catalyst that led to the development of strong military ties between Ethiopia and the Soviet Union. It speeded up the creation of an ideological and military relationship, and led to vibrant ties between Ethiopia and other socialist states. Ethiopia's national interest in preserving its geographical integrity in the face of a massive Somali invasion converged with Soviet national interests. This convergence led to a close ideological relationship as the Soviets could see directly how revolutionary the Mengistu regime was within a Marxist-Leninist framework. 'In seeking a relationship with the Soviet Union, Ethiopia . . . aimed primarily at obtaining political recognition as a revolutionary country' (Ottaway, 1982, pp. 157-8). Clearly, Ethiopia achieved its goals. The Soviet Union too has accomplished its objectives within the context of its strategic and ideological interests. Although the Soviet Union tried to get Somalia and Ethiopia to work out their territorial problem within a peaceful and socialist international framework, Somalia, greedy for 'its' territory and believing that it could take advantage of the internal chaos in Ethiopia, tried to settle the issue with a blitzkrieg war. It failed, but it set the stage for an Ethiopian-Soviet alliance that has benefited both countries. Its action, unfortunately, also led to a massive refugee problem that is still unsettled. Some 700,000 Ethiopians from the Ogaden fled to Somalia, most being ethnic Somalis who clearly were not opposed to Somalia's cause. Unofficial statistics maintain that 1.2 million refugees are now living in camps in Somalia (*Report of the UN High Commission for Refugees*, 1982, pp. 24-5). Up to 1981 the United Nations had expended $49,078,164 to help Somalia care for these displaced persons (ibid.). Had Somalia not invaded Ethiopia, this extraordinary situation, which is the worst refugee problem in the world, would not have existed. Another aspect of the problem is the tragedy in the Ogaden itself. Ethiopian troops, who, along with the Ethiopian government, believed that the Ogaden Somalis were to a large degree collaborators, inflicted heavy damage and killed many Somalis when the Ogaden was retaken. As a result many had no villages or homes to return to. The United Nations has allocated to Ethiopia since 1978 $7.9 million in humanitarian aid so that life in the Ogaden can be restored to normal (ibid.,p. 22).

In terms of Ethiopia's relationship with the Soviet bloc, 1977 must be considered a watershed year. For with the invasion of the Ogaden, Ethiopia firmed up its foreign policy in that it moved away from the

United States and constructed a foreign policy framework that both conceptually and in practice tied in close to the Soviet Union and other socialist states. Cuba and the Soviet Union, most particularly, rushed to Ethiopia's aid and were the key actors in preserving the geographical sanctity of Ethiopia. The relationship with both states remains close, despite the alleged Soviet pressure upon Ethiopia quickly to establish a vanguard political party. Mengistu has fashioned a foreign policy that ties Ethiopia very closely to the Soviet Union while at the same time tries to disallow the Soviets from making Ethiopia a purely client state. The Soviet Union has attained many of its objectives in Ethiopia and the Horn of Africa, while it has not attained them all. Ethiopia obtained its immediate objective in the Ogaden, and the long-run object of creating a framework that ensures continued ties to the socialist commonwealth. Thus, regionally and within the international cold war, the Soviet Union has attained its strategic ambition; as for Ethiopia it has been accepted as a truly revolutionary state that has been integrated more than any other African state has ever been into the socialist commonwealth of nations, and at the same time it retained its control over the Ogaden. Both achieved their immediate and long-term ends. The convergence of their national and international interests was the primary variable in this circumstance. As a result Ethiopia with its armed forces of 300,000 has become the major state in the region of the Horn of Africa and to a very great degree sets the diplomatic framework to which all other states in the region have to respond. Although Ethiopia's foreign policy was not planned out thoughtfully and over time, but was forced upon it, its outcome, at least in the near term, has been triumphant.

The International Aspects of the War in Eritrea

Eritrea, which gives Ethiopia access to the Red Sea, has an area of 119,000 sq. km. and a population of about two million, of whom some 56 per cent are Muslim. Eritrea was captured by Italy in 1890 and became part of Italian East Africa in 1936. It was occupied by British forces in the spring of 1941 and from then on was administered by the United Kingdom. On 2 December 1950 the UN General Assembly passed a resolution by a vote of 46–10 recommending that Eritrea should 'constitute an autonomous unit federated with Ethiopia under sovereignty of the Ethiopian crown'. The Federal government was to control defence, foreign affairs, finance, foreign and interstate commerce, and external and interstate communications, including ports. The resolution envisaged common citizenship and an Imperial Federal Council with Eritrean and Ethiopian representation. The Eritrean government was to have legislative, executive and judicial power in the field of domestic affairs and to be responsible for all matters not under the jurisdiction of the Federal government. On 16 September 1952 Britain formally handed over Eritrea to Ethiopia. In May 1960 the central government at Addis Ababa announced that the Eritrean government would henceforth be known as the Eritrean Administration. On 14 November 1962, Eritrea was formally incorporated into Ethiopia as one of its fourteen regions (for an excellent work on the subject see Sherman, 1980).

In 1953, at a time when neither Somalia nor Djibouti were independent, the US signed a mutual-defence treaty with Ethiopia which laid the basis for the modernization of the Ethiopian military, and was to be used to maintain Ethiopia's internal security, its self-defence, and to permit the United States to participate in the defence of the area. After the British withdrawal from Eritrea, the United States realized the vulnerability of the area around the Horn of Africa, and, with the defence treaty as a basis, moved quickly to fill the vacuum. To 1974 the United States provided Ethiopia with half the military assistance it provided to all African states. In support of its policy objectives a United States Military Assistance Advisory Group was attached to the Ethiopian Ministry of Defence in 1953 and in the same year Kagnew, an American base, was opened near Asmara, Eritrea. It eventually quartered 3,200 of the 6,000 US military personnel in Ethiopia (*US Security Agreements*, 1970). Its functions included allowing US military forces access to the Red Sea and providing support to Ethiopia in its battle against Eritrean insurgents opting for secession (*A History of Kagnew Station and American Forces in Eritrea*, 1973). When the secessionist battle began in 1962 the United States sent in counter-insurgent teams, increased its military aid programme, and expanded its modernization and training programme for the Ethiopian military (*US Security Agreements*, op. cit.).

At the same time Israel, fearful of a Muslim Eritrea that might act with other Muslim-Arab states to close off the Red Sea, initiated its own aid programme in Ethiopia. Ethiopian commando units and security personnel were trained by the Israelis and they established for the Ethiopians a communications network in Eritrea that enabled the Ethiopian military to be more effective in its military operations. [Schwab, 1979, p. 95.]

Massawa and Assab are the only outlets to the sea that Ethiopia has access to within its own territory. Djibouti, which became independent from France in June 1977, offers another avenue to the sea. A railroad line between Addis Ababa and the port of Djibouti has existed since 1917. Since the mid-1960s, when the war with Eritrea became intense, some 40-60 per cent of Ethiopia's exports and imports have flowed through Djibouti, although this avenue has often been curtailed by insurgent Somali activity as a result of which the railroad line has often been severed.

> In so far as foreign policy is concerned, Ethiopia (under Haile Selassie) . . . viewed the crisis in Eritrea and its relationship with Djibouti through one lens. When the Eritrean Liberation Front began its secessionist movement in 1962 Haile Selassie immediately reacted by sending in armed forces. There was to be no consideration of separatist demands for independence. As the Ethiopian/Eritrean war increased in scope and violence the military was reinforced and by 1965 some 50 per cent of the Ethiopian army—20,000 troops—were stationed or fighting in Eritrea. [Schwab, 1978, p. 14.]

Haile Selassie was unwilling to permit Ethiopia once again to revert to a land-locked status and thus his policy, which was consistently applied, was militarily to destroy the insurgents. By 1974 the Eritrean rebels had taken well over 95 per cent of Eritrea 'and there can no longer be any serious hope of defeating the rebels by military force' (Sherman, 1980, p. 83). Yet, Eritrea was still under Ethiopian authority, weak as it was, when the Dergue took power.

The secessionist movement in Eritrea has almost from the beginning been involved in its own civil strife. This has led to splits within the movement and a deterioration of its position, often when it was on the verge of victory. The schisms 'increased the competition for power and petty political jealousies. While the Eritreans bickered amongst themselves . . . the Ethiopian army exploited the . . . differences to the fullest. . . . [A] war of words and bullets continued to escalate among the . . . liberation organizations' (ibid., pp. 43, 45).

The ELF, a largely Muslim organization initially supported also by young Christian intellectuals, came into being in 1962. In 1970 it split into two separate entities, the ELF-Revolutionary Council and the Eritrean People's Liberation Front (EPLF). The ELF-Revolutionary Council desires self-determination for Eritrea, and until 1977 demanded recognition as the sole representative of the Eritrean people (ELF, 1971). The EPLF split off from the ELF because of ideological and organizational differences. Its objectives include the establishment of a people's democracy with a planned national economy, the nationalization of all land and industry, the integration of the Eritrean nationality, and support for all revolutionary movements in Africa (EPLF, 1977). The EPLF is the more precise in terms of its ideology, and it is ideology rather than religious differences that set it apart from the ELF. 'From the very beginning, the ELF followed a line . . . based on competitive feudal sentiments' (ibid., p. 9). The EPLF is socialist, without religious orientation, while the ELF-Revolutionary Council views itself as an organization whose essential values lie in Islam.

In 1976 the EPLF itself split, when the Secretary-General, Osman Saleh Sabbe, was thrown out by those elements of the EPLF who believed that he had been sowing a 'reactionary line' by his attempt in 1975 to establish unity with the ELF. In 1976, with the financial support of Saudi Arabia, he established the ELF-Popular Liberation Forces—smaller in terms of adherents than either of the other two liberation movements, it is also far more conservative, though it too demands secession from Ethiopia. In late 1977 the EPLF and the ELF-Revolutionary Council created a united front and in 1978 maintained that they would crush the ELF-Popular Liberation Forces unless it absorbed itself into the front. The ELF-Popular Liberation Forces refused, and the civil strife among the various forces continues.

Thus, when the Dergue came to power it was faced with an extremely complex issue. Cuba and the Soviet Union were supporters of the EPLF, the EPLF was a socialist entity, Eritrea was the site of Ethiopia's only direct outlets to the sea, and in addition to a secessionist war, civil strife within the Eritrean liberation movements was rampant. Along with Cuba and the Soviet Union, the Eritreans were supported by Saudi Arabia, the Sudan, Libya, South Yemen, Iraq and Syria. On the Ethiopian side were Israel, fearful of the Red Sea becoming an 'Arab lake', the United States, and nominally the People's Republic of China. The international array of actors was uncharacteristic of the traditional cold war line-up and complicated matters even further for the Dergue when it began to consider its Eritrean policy.

Having withstood twelve years against Haile Selassie's army and with Eritrea under its virtual control the ELF, together with the EPLF, were convinced that the Dergue would be far more sympathetic to their objectives. This was particularly so of the EPLF whose ideology was very much in tune with the philosophy of the Dergue. But, both the ELF and the EPLF were mistaken.

Aman Michael Andon, who ruled the Dergue in the first months after the takeover, believed that a negotiated settlement was the only way out of the Eritrean quagmire. But his execution in November 1974 put an end to any possibility of negotiation within the near future. Teferi Banti and Mengistu, the primary subsequent figures in the Dergue, accepted the doctrine that permitting Eritrea to obtain independence would cause the disintegration of the country.

Haile Selassie's policy toward Eritrea and Djibouti was adopted in full. 'The Djibouti/Eritrean connection as regards outlets to the sea [was to be] kept intact by the junta. Ethiopia must have its own ports. Eritrea was to be maintained as part of Ethiopia and Djibouti was to be kept from Somalia' which looked to Djibouti as another one of its 'lost' territories (Schwab, 1978, p. 16).

Unfortunately for Ethiopia the military government was unable successfully to carry out its policy. The Somali push into the Ogaden, together with the internal unrest in the cities, forced Ethiopia into a three-front war, in Eritrea, the Ogaden and against the EPRP. With the loss of American weapons due to President Ford's sharp restriction of military aid to Ethiopia, and the armed forces too thinly spread out, Ethiopian troops were sent reeling. By 1977 only Asmara, Massawa and Assab were controlled by the government; Eritrea was basically under the authority of the insurgents. Part of Ethiopia's military problems in Eritrea were due to the extraordinary political contradictions inherent in its military policy. As an advocate of socialism, recognition of national distinctions is contrary to its ideology, yet, as the 1976 ENDRP makes clear, differing nationalities were recognized.

On 16 May, one month after the ENDRP was made public, the Dergue unveiled its Nine-Point Peace Plan for Eritrea. It called on progressive Eritrean forces to unite with Ethiopia in order to achieve the goals of the revolution. Point 2, however, affirmed 'the right of self-determination of nationalities through regional autonomy which takes due account of objective realities prevailing in Ethiopia'. The plan also called for full participation by the Eritreans in the life of Ethiopia, urged negotiations with progressive Eritreans, and declared that Eritrea would be rehabilitated after the establishment of peace. Berhanu Bayih, who was charged with the responsibility of pursuing an Eritrean settlement along the lines of the Peace Plan, claimed that autonomy was the only way of dealing with the nationalities issue. 'We believe that recognition of each nationality's right to self-determination and regional autonomy is the correct way to solve the nationalities question in line with socialist principles and Ethiopia's objective conditions' (Berhanu Bayih, 1978, pp. 54–5). The conflict inherent in recognizing autonomy while pursuing the strategy of destroying the ELF and EPLF by military force appeared to produce a political paralysis that even the sharply divided insurgents were able to take advantage of.

In 1977 however the contradiction was finally resolved. Though still giving lip-service to the Peace Plan's claim of autonomy the Dergue adopted Lenin's dictum that 'the proletariat cannot support any consecration of nationalism; on the contrary, it supports everything that helps to obliterate national distinctions and remove national barriers; it supports everything that . . . tends to merge nations. To act differently means siding with reactionary philistinism' (Lenin, 1970, p. 28). As Lenin's theories were used by the Dergue to impose socialism from above, violently if necessary, so too were they applied to the Eritrean issue. Full military force, without quarter, was to be used against the insurgents. This time however a new element was present. The Soviet Union, Cuba, Libya and South Yemen switched sides, eliminated their previous support of the Eritreans, and lent aid to the Ethiopian government to be used in Eritrea.

As part of Soviet strategy to shore up its naval facilities and to strengthen its strategic position on the Red Sea/Indian Ocean, it moved rapidly to reinforce its position in Ethiopia that was initiated during the Somali invasion. In its continuing effort to reduce United States' influence in the area, hoping to attain base facilities at the ports of Massawa and Assab, and to demonstrate 'that the Soviet Union has world power . . . to carry out its intentions' (Sherman, 1980, p. 149), the Soviet Union linked up with a viable revolutionary state and moved against its former allies in Eritrea. In September 1977 delivery of MIG-jet fighters, T-54 and T-55 tanks, helicopters, and small-arms were trans-shipped by air to

Ethiopia to be used in the Eritrean campaign. At the same time, 3,500 Cuban military personnel, backed by Soviet logistics, flew combat missions against the Eritreans, and were used as ground support and back-up troops to the Ethiopians. While Cuba does owe a massive debt to the Soviet Union because of its dependence on Soviet aid, its involvement in Ethiopia is probably due as much to Castro's belief in the Ethiopian revolution as 'a genuinely progressive force' (ibid., p. 152). After the Somalia-Ethiopia war was concluded the full energies of Cuba, Ethiopia and the Soviet Union were turned against Eritrea; by 1979 the Eritreans were reeling in retreat, having been overwhelmed by superior military force. Eritrea became a virtual free-fire zone, with constant bombing from the air (including the partial destruction of Asmara) and continuous ground attacks. The Cuban-Soviet-Ethiopian alliance destroyed the effectiveness of the ELF and EPLF. And although a large Ethiopian/Cuban garrison remains in Eritrea, and fighting continues, though on a level far less intense, the secessionist movement has, at least in the short term, been vanquished. The Dergue had moved to 'obliterate national distinctions' in Eritrea via the barrel of the gun. And although the national distinctions have not been eliminated, the ELF and EPLF, for all effective purposes, have.

The Soviets, Cubans and Ethiopians achieved their short- and long-term objectives. In addition to its facilities in the Dahlak Islands the Soviets were permitted by Ethiopia to build an airbase at Makele, Tigre, just south of Eritrea. MIG-21 and MIG-23 jets are based there, as are Russian and Cuban pilots. Also transferred there when the base was completed in 1981 were the Soviet helicopter fleet, T-55 and T-62 tanks along with their South Yemen crews (Sherman, ibid., p. 93). The Soviets have attained air and sea power on the Horn and directly on the Red Sea that places them in a superior position *vis-à-vis* the United States in that region. Their position on the Indian Ocean and the Gulf of Aden has been strengthened markedly. From the Ogaden war and the Eritrean insurgency the Soviet Union has attained its strategic objectives. In so doing it has also developed its relationship further with revolutionary Ethiopia. Cuba, which has acquired a military base in Debre Zeit, south of Addis Ababa, has expanded its position with revolutionary states by its action in Ethiopia. This, of course, is very much in line with Castro's philosophy to support all true revolutionary states. As for Ethiopia, it destroyed the position of the insurgents, took control of Eritrea to a greater extent than any government has been able to since 1962, and further consolidated its connection with the Soviet Union. Ideologically and politically Ethiopia's domestic and foreign policy objectives were met. The rewards to the Soviet Union and Cuba were necessary, given their astounding role in the Eritrean (and in the Ogaden) struggle. As Sherman put it:

> With this sort of firepower and foreign personnel . . . it is easy to understand how . . . the Eritrean guerrilla forces could be forced to retreat. By November [1978] most of the major towns were again under Ethiopian control. The 1978 Ethiopian assault was, for the most part, engineered by the Soviets and carried out by Ethiopian, Cuban, and South Yemeni forces. Soviet and East German engineers . . . built flanking roads for the Ethiopian tanks to come up behind Eritrean lines. The Eritreans were caught in a pincer thrust by tank forces crewed by Ethiopians and Cubans, supported by artillery and rocket units operated by East Germans and South Yemenis. [Ibid.]

Ethiopian foreign policy has of necessity concentrated, ironically, on areas considered by the state to be integral parts of the country. Opponents however disagree, maintaining that both Eritrea and the Ogaden were imperialized by Ethiopia. The insurgents and Somalia view 'their' respective regions from an international perspective. Ethiopia has been forced to do the same. In shaping and conducting its foreign policy in both areas Ethiopia has been very successful. It has succeeded in defeating the Somalis and the ELF/EPLF, allowing it to hold on to both the Ogaden and Eritrea. Through its policy it developed a striking and powerful relationship with the Soviet Union, the bloc countries, Cuba and South Yemen. With the Soviet Union it has played a role in sharply curtailing the United States' role in and around the Horn of Africa, and has helped to create the conditions whereby the United States has to react to the very potent tenure of the Soviet Union. That the Soviet Union, Cuba and Ethiopia had national and international interests that converged in time and place was beneficial to Ethiopia. It allowed it to strengthen its ties to the socialist commonwealth while at the same time permitted it to maintain its territorial integrity.

Only since 1980 has Ethiopia been in the position of being able to establish traditional diplomatic and political links with other socialist states, and as stated above, it is doing so. With the Ogaden and Eritrea receding in terms of day-to-day concern, Ethiopia no longer has to monopolize its foreign policy energies in that direction. It can be also expected that in the future more traditional diplomatic activity with non-socialist states in the area of foreign affairs will occur. Still, this will be limited to the degree that the United States, particularly under President Reagan, insists on invoking an aggressive stance toward Soviet and Cuban involvement on the Horn. Chester Crocker, Reagan's Assistant Secretary of State for African Affairs, informed the Council on Foreign Relations, 5 October, 1981, that 'it is . . . time to recognize . . . that the solution to regional disputes does not lie in Western abstinence at a time when Libyan, Soviet and Cuban policies seek actively to exploit and fuel the fires of instability' (Rothchild & Ravenhill, 1983, p. 349). If such a destructive engagement is maintained it can almost be predicted that Ethiopia will be forced to move ever closer to the Soviet Union. And though it has been established that Ethiopia wishes to keep some distance between itself and the Soviets, its leadership has established a close working relationship with its superpower ally, and would not be completely averse to strengthening those ties. Ethiopia is presently moving to acquire economic aid from the United States in its effort to shore up the domestic economy. If however the Crocker philosophy is adhered to, such aid will most probably be denied and Ethiopia's connection to the socialist bloc will increase significantly. Given Soviet reluctance to supply economic aid this would not be in Ethiopia's best interest; but if the United States locks Ethiopia out of aid packages because of Cuban/Soviet involvement, then Ethiopia will have little choice but to try to work through the East European Council for Mutual Economic Assistance (CMEA). Ethiopia already attends its meetings and benefits minimally from its programmes. However, due to the severe strains caused by declining economic growth rates, unsatisfactory productivity, inflation, consumer shortages, debt and uncertain energy supplies, the East European bloc can offer little to countries like Ethiopia. But, if the United States remains adamant in its opposition to states like Ethiopia, then Ethiopia will have to be satisfied with what benefits it can obtain from CMEA. To a large degree Ethiopia's future foreign policy direction will be framed by the position of the United States and the Soviet Union and their relations with one another. Ethiopia would prefer to deal economically with the United States and the West, and militarily, politically and ideologically with the Soviet Union and the Eastern bloc. Whether or not this is possible is a function of the world economy and Soviet/United States relations. That, however, is the direction that is apparently preferred by Mengistu and Dergue/COPWE. Ethiopia's role in pursuing this policy is marginal. Although a major regional actor, it is still very much a country of the Third World, and its ability to determine its own future is limited by international forces it has little control over.

Ethiopia's position in the Third World has been strengthened by its marked success in the Ogaden and Eritrea. Noting the importance of Ethiopia, the OAU, meeting in Addis Ababa in June 1983, selected Mengistu as chairman of the Organization for 1983–4. It was clear vindication of Mengistu's policies and verification of his position among African leaders. It indicated very strongly that Mengistu was moving away from the concentration forced upon him by events in the north and south-east of Ethiopia, and to an enlarged African presence. Ethiopia's foreign policy would henceforth be within the frame of a socialist state allied closely to the Soviet bloc, but would try to edge closer to the West economically, and would integrate itself far more with the affairs of Africa. Mengistu's role as chairman of the OAU gave him the opportunity via prestige and platform to universalize Ethiopia's foreign policy network.

5 Conclusion

Certainly, since the onset of the revolution in 1974 much controversy has surrounded the tactics and policies of socialist Ethiopia. This is primarily reflected through the criticism that has swirled around the terror imposed on its enemies by Mengistu's government, the establishment of a socialist construct by a relatively small cadre of military junior officers, the decision to maintain the geographical integrity of Ethiopia and the concurrent policy of disallowing Eritrean secession, and the use of Cuban troops and Soviet advisers to oust Somali forces from the Ogaden. Through all the dissent and counter-revolutionary activity the leaders of Dergue/COPWE have been clear as to their direction and 'line of march'. As a result of their vision, Ethiopia's leaders have never shifted from their radical ideals. They imposed their theories, and defeated and eliminated the opposition. The country is now poised to develop its support so as to further enhance socialist values. It is at a stage of equilibrium where the preconditions are in place for the establishment of a vanguard party, and the rapid establishment of an orthodox socialist state (see p. 62).

The acceptance of orthodoxy however should not detract from the originality of the Ethiopian revolution. In its originality can be found much of the importance of the revolution itself. It has, to some degree, led to the creation of a new ideal-type of socialist revolution for the Third World. There is no doubt that the success of Ethiopia's leftist revolutionaries has led other socialist revolutionaries to adopt similar styles of rule and policies of state. Perhaps the most notable example of this is in Liberia where in April 1980 a *coup d'état* led by Master Sergeant Samuel K. Doe overthrew the Americo-Liberian government led by William Tolbert. Most of the old guard were either executed or thrown into prison and the traditional ideology and political structures were eliminated. At the present time a constitution is being written in Liberia to institutionalize the new political order. One primary difference between the two countries however is that in Liberia the intellectual community quickly threw its support behind the new government. In fact, Amos Sawyerr, the Dean of the University of Liberia in Monrovia, and one of the most politically astute intellectuals is co-ordinating the writing of the new charter. The United States, however, is attempting to use its economic leverage to prevent Liberia from adopting the Ethiopian model. So clearly, the ideological underpinnings of the Ethiopian revolution and the sucess of the revolutionaries have led to a new political equation in Africa and the Third World. Mengistu commented on this subject at a news conference in Addis Ababa on 15 February 1978:

> In general, the basic and essential laws of revolution have worked for Ethiopia. [However] there are certain situations which make the Ethiopian Revolution different from other revolutions. What does set the Ethiopian revolution apart from other revolutions is the ability to introduce drastic measures without a proletarian party and still manage to foil subversive activity. The fact that the armed forces which were molded under a feudo-bourgeois system have until now stood and struggled with the democratic revolution of the broad masses is the other novel aspect of our revolution. [Addis Ababa Domestic Service, 15 February 1978.]

Events in Liberia, where there have been direct references to 'comrades' in Ethiopia, and the praise heaped upon Ethiopia's leaders by Fidel Castro, clearly indicate that Ethiopia has developed a new revolutionary framework that others are looking to.

It is also evident that Mengistu will soon move to create an orthodox vanguard political party. At the same news conference he stated that 'it can easily be seen that even now Ethiopia's communist forces are engaged in a committed struggle to . . . establish a proletarian party in order to ensure the proletarian dictatorship. A reliable foundation has been laid for the establishment of the Party'. Mengistu's desire to integrate orthodoxy with originality was specified in his concluding statements at the news conference.

> There are areas of activity which justify us in saying that Lenin's great lessons in militancy and leadership have served us well. Making decisions promptly and without hesitation or constraint can be counted as decisive factors for the triumph of our revolution. That is to say, that the anti-people forces who had lined us up for their lunch—we have had them for breakfast.

In confronting opponents in the cities, in Eritrea and the Ogaden, and in its dealings with the United States, Ethiopia has been defiant but enormously successful. Politically, the leadership of Ethiopia has taken the country a long way. The old feudal order has been completely destroyed, a new ideology based on socialism has been developed with a corresponding political order created and institutionalized. Peasants and the urban proletariat are finally, and fortunately, obtaining their primary human and social, political and economic needs. The country is more unified and more at peace with itself than it has been for decades. The Eritrean problem has been largely resolved, the Ogaden is slowly being reintegrated, and internal opponents are impotent. Politically, Ethiopia is truly at a take-off stage where it can move quickly to solidify socialism and socialist values.

Economically, however, it is another story. Although peasants now have access to land that they never had, agricultural output is growing far too slowly and much needs to be done if the agricultural economy is to support its population in anything other than subsistence form. With drought, a stagnating Gross Domestic Product, the slowing of exports, and its increasing imbalance of trade, Ethiopia's economic position is very shaky. At the same time inflation is reducing the purchasing power of Ethiopians.

Although much of its economic stagnation results from high oil prices, the worldwide recession (for the Third World clearly a depression), and the decline in world prices for coffee, much of it is also due to the political turmoil caused by the radical and speedy land reform programme. The countryside was turned upside-down by the implementation of land reform, and although it was politically necessary, it caused a certain amount of economic havoc. Now that the country is relatively calm and the turmoil is over, greater concentration must be given to organizing the collectives and farmers so as to increase agricultural productivity. With the political order stabilized, the economic order under socialism can be more adequately constructed. The political prerequisites have been met, which in a socialist state is a necessary precondition for economic growth. As Paul Baran maintained, 'the establishment of a socialist planned economy is an essential, indeed indispensable, condition for the attainment of economic and social progress in underdeveloped countries' (Baran, 1957, p. 261). He felt compelled to clarify his assumption:

> The task confronting a socialist revolution in a backward country is much more complex. It must not merely generate a vast development of the country's productive forces. It must also—in order to accomplish this—create the altogether new economic and social order of socialism. 'The bourgeois revolution *terminates* usually with the conquest of power, while for the proletarian revolution the conquest of power

represents merely its beginning, with power employed as a leverage for the reconstruction of the old economy and the organization of the new'. [Ibid., pp. 261, 262. His quote is from Stalin, 1948, p. 21.]

Both Baran and Stalin might well have been speaking of contemporary Ethiopia. In terms of Ethiopia's economy, Baran's analysis holds true and it is now timely for Dergue/COPWE to employ its power to satisfactorily organize and stabilize the Ethiopian economy. And if the Soviet Union will not or cannot assist Ethiopia to develop economically, then it is incumbent upon the leadership to seek out other sources that will aid it but will do so upon Ethiopia's terms that will of course lie within its revolutionary and socialist framework. For Ethiopia this means primarily that agriculture must be included in the

> general nexus of the national economy . . . by liquidating subsistence farming . . . and transforming agriculture into a specializing, labour-dividing, and market-oriented industry in which the structure of output as well as its distribution . . . can be determined by the planning authority, as in the case of other industries. Under conditions of socialism this transformation cannot be accomplished except by means of productive cooperation of the peasants, through collectivization of peasant farming . . . [ibid., p. 268].

In terms of manufactures Ethiopia, as detailed above, ought to concentrate on further developing small-scale industry orientated to a domestic market. This makes the most sense given Ethiopia's agriculturism. Even a small increase in its minor industrial capacity will help it to limit imports, reduce its balance of payments deficit, and increase its domestic urban employment. Greater self-reliance will only add proletarian support for the state. One of the political banners carried at rallies in Addis Ababa says 'Ethiopia will not be a second Chile'. Less dependence on imported goods can help to create reality out of rhetoric.

Whether or not Ethiopia moves closer to or further away from the Soviet international fabric, there is little doubt that unless a successful counter-revolutionary attack occurs (which appears extremely doubtful), Ethiopia and the Soviet Union will continue a close alliance. Anwar el-Sadat's model in Egypt will not recur in Ethiopia under Dergue/COPWE. It is likely that in the short term Ethiopia will be driven to firm up its connection to the Soviet Union. Given the present United States' policy advanced by President Ronald Reagan that sees El Salvador, Nicaragua, Cuba, Angola and Ethiopia as all linked to the Soviet centre, his 'confrontationist policies toward radical states may drive them closer to the Soviet Union' (Oye, 1983, p. 20; see also Reagan's 27 April 1983 speech on Central America before a joint session of the US Congress). Even though Ethiopia may work out more extensive bilateral trade agreements with Western European states, its reliance upon the Soviet Union for military aid, and its ideological parallels with Cuba and the Soviet Union, will only serve to reinforce the Ethiopian-Cuban-Soviet connection. Certainly *vis-à-vis* Western aid the 'relationship between external economic policy and internal political and economic ideology appears to be diminishing' (ibid.). It is however to be expected that solidarity among Ethiopia and its sister socialist states will continue to expand.

Ethiopia has come through a prodigious nationalist uprising that is astonishing in its effect. To be clear, it was a revolution based on national values. The ideology expounded by its leadership, however, thrust it firmly within the socialist camp and led to political, ideological and economic linkage with the socialist commonwealth. Thus, rooted in nationalism the Ethiopian revolution concurrently adopted socialism, predicated on Lenin's and Stalin's interpretation, as both its means and ends. From the beginning the revolution was both nationalist and socialist. As such it was remarkably similar to the nationalist and socialist uprising in Vietnam that led to the defeat of French colonialism, United States' imperialism, and Western indigenous client governments. Both countries are closely allied with the Soviet Union, yet each is nationalist in its approach. There is no contradiction between nationalism and socialism as both blend together so that national needs match socialist goals.

Ethiopia's revolution is to be praised. Those who bore witness to the repression and to the political system that locked out everyone but the elite prior to 1974 can see that extraordinary and positive changes have taken place. For many observers and intellectuals it has been impossible to support Mengistu's policies because of the methods used to implant the revolutionary political order. Almost two decades ago a prescient political philosopher predicted what the response to such a revolt would be and also articulated the revolutionary answer to such critics.

> The leftist [critic] tried in vain to explain actions which seemed incomprehensible, shocking and politically absurd. For example, the death of children, and persons outside of the struggle. . . . That it could be the cruelty of oppression which explained the blind fury of the reaction hardly seemed to be an argument to him.

> What! [revolutionaries] tell him, a people is waiting, suffering from hunger, illness and contempt, one child in four dies before he is one year old, and he wants assurance on means and ends! What conditions he sets for his co-operation! After all, this matter is one of ethics and ideology. [Memmi, 1967, pp. 30–1, 35.]

Although one may reasonably understand why those intellectuals who opposed the Dergue did so with such vehemence, this author agrees with Memmi, and also with Fidel Castro who in 1975 proclaimed the Ethiopian revolution to be 'of great interest and historic importance' (quoted in Halliday & Molyneux, 1981, p. 252). The aspects of the revolution that critics have used to justify their attacks appear to have been necessary. The centrifugal tendencies set in motion throughout 1974 required severe policies that would cohere the various forces that could not or would not function in a unified fashion.

> The irony of the Ethiopian revolution was that this most radical of revolutions from above owed its revolutionary transformation to the crisis of Ethiopian society and the force of the movement for change. The new military rulers felt compelled to crush those competitors for power who had helped create the conditions in which they sought power and to do so with comparably greater ferocity. The force of the terror [indicated] the degree to which revolutions from above are prepared by mass actions from below, and the degree to which they then have to assert control over their precursors. [Ibid., p. 31.]

The same perspective should be used in measuring Mengistu's value to the revolution. His leadership, from the onset of the revolution, mirrored Lenin's theoretical outlook. Lenin maintained that 'the revolutionary dictatorship of the proletariat is rule won and maintained by the use of violence by the proletariat against the bourgeoisie, rule that is unrestricted by any laws' (Lenin, 1968, p. 365). Accepting this premise Mengistu adopted the means advocated by Lenin and Stalin to achieve Marxist-Leninist goals. For socialism to emerge from a lengthy and solidified tradition of feudalism required the ruthlessness and vision that Mengistu displayed. In 1977 the noted scholar I. M. Lewis proclaimed that Mengistu's 'clumsy and brutal' imposition of authority would lead to the destruction and dismemberment of Ethiopia and that not only would Ethiopia lose Eritrea and the Ogaden but that not 'much of Ethiopia will remain' (Lewis, 1977). Despite the similar words of most critics of that time, it was precisely the cold-blooded assessment of events, and the severe implementation of authority that both kept Ethiopia whole and permitted socialist values to emerge intact and vigorous. Lewis and the others were wrong; Lenin was correct. In a situation such as that which existed in Ethiopia, only the violence of the proletariat and the peasantry can certify the success of a socialist revolution. Mengistu was accurate in his appraisal and correct in his remedy. He has not only been of great value to the success of the revolution; it is possible that the revolution would have degenerated into civil war without his presence. Such civil strife may well have destroyed the revolution at birth, obliterated Ethiopia's geographical integrity, and permitted a non-socialist military junta with close ties to the old feudal aristocracy to emerge. Mengistu is a 'true revolutionary [directing] a true revolution' (Castro, 1977, p. 16). He has not only been extremely successful in prodding Ethiopia in the direction of socialism; he has been a vital figure whose value to the revolution has been immense. Rather than being a political innocent, he has been astute and clever. He has been a consistently true believer in the need to establish socialist values and he has done whatever has been necessary to achieve success. In retrospect, his stance has been accurate and without deviation.

Mengistu, who was born in 1941 in Addis Ababa, came from peasant class origins, and the minor ethnic community, the Shankella. Although his heritage is traced from his mother, his father was an Amhara soldier who eventually came to work for Ras Kebede Tessema, an important aristocrat. At the age of seventeen, he became a cadet at Holeta, graduating as a second lieutenant in 1959. He was then posted to the Third Army position. He later travelled to the United States where he studied industrial economics at the University of Maryland. According to *Granma* (22 January 1978) his experience with racism and the incipient United States involvement in Vietnam left him bitter, but developed his political insights. In December 1960, Mengistu took part in the abortive coup staged by Haile Selassie's Imperial Guard. The emperor spared him for his political activities, and the pardon was every bit as fatal to Haile Selassie's regime as was the Tsar's leniency toward some Bolshevik leaders to imperial rule in Russia, and decided the course of the revolution much as Fulgencio Batista's decision not to execute Fidel Castro decided the future of Cuba.

Mengistu is extremely well-versed in the history and culture of Ethiopia and often uses his knowledge in speeches, rallies and conferences.

There is no doubt that the revolution would have taken a different turn without him, and that he has altered the history of Ethiopia. In 1980 Mengistu, in recognition of his role, was decorated by the General Secretary of the Communist party of the Soviet Union, Leonid Brezhnev, with the Order of the October Revolution. An impressive programme was put on for Mengistu by Brezhnev at Alma-Ata, a region similar to Ethiopia. Mengistu's 30-year-old wife and three children attended. There can be little doubt left that Mengistu was, and continues to be, the spearhead of the revolution. Whatever happens in the future, he has carved an original niche into the historical tradition of socialism. He has been the engine of the revolution and deserves to be given much of the credit for its success.

In 1984, ten years after the removal of the Haile Selassie government, Ethiopia has moved light years away from the once-powerful feudal autocracy. Socialist construction has been developed, the social, political and economic structure has been transformed, and society functions within the constraints established by socialist ideology. It is remarkable that the change occurred at all given the apparent solidity of traditional feudalism. The first ten years of the revolution ensure that the future of the country will be very different from its past. Ethiopia has the potential to become an important and vital segment of the Third World in much the same way that Cuba has. In terms of its ideology and its policies it can serve as a beacon, or more correctly as a paradigm. Despite the contemporary problems that still exist, the Ethiopian case provides an extraordinary example of what socialism can achieve in a conservative, apparently unchanging, traditional, feudal state. The revolution has brought to the Ethiopian peasant and proletariat a future; something neither group had prior to 1974.

However socialist Ethiopia develops, people who once belonged to the lowest strata of the Ethiopian social structure now have hope that their lives, and the lives of their children can flourish in ways that were impossible in the past. Change was never seen as likely in a feudal system that thrived on maintaining the social status quo. With the revolution hope was reborn, change was experienced, and a promising future became a feature of society. It offered to Ethiopians of the once-oppressed classes 'an association, in which the free development of each is the condition for the free development of all' (Marx, Engels, 1848). This freedom, imposed in Rousseauean and Leninist terms, is finally what the

Ethiopian revolution was, and is, all about. Ethiopia is in the process of becoming fully liberated, in that

> economic, political, and cultural features of a classless society . . . have become the basic needs of those who fight for it. . . . The initial institutions of liberation . . . collective ownership, collective control and planning of the means of production and distribution . . . make possible the usage of all available resources for the abolition of poverty which is the prerequisite for . . . quantity to quality. [Marcuse, 1969, pp. 88–9, 87.]

Ethiopia, politically, now has the potential to meet the uplifted expectations of its once-exploited classes. There is no fundamental reason for the state not to continue to move in this direction. The movement or lack of it will, in the final analysis, determine the intrinsic success or failure of the revolution.

Bibliography

Addis Ababa Domestic (Radio) Service 1978. 15 February.

— 1983. 25 March.

— 1981. 1 May.

Africa Confidential. 1981. 11 March.

A History of Kagnew Station and American Forces in Eritrea, 1973. Arlington, Information Division IACS-I, Headquarters, US Army Security Agency.

Amnesty International 1977. *Ethiopia: The Human Rights Situation*. London.

— 1978. *Human Rights Violations in Ethiopia*. London.

An Observer 1977. 'Revolution in Ethiopia'. *Monthly Review*, vol. 29, July-August.

Baran, P. A. 1957. *The Political Economy of Growth*. New York, Prometheus.

Baxter, P. T. W. 1978. 'Ethiopia's Unacknowledged Problem: The Oromo', *African Affairs*, vol. 77, no. 308.

Bayih, B. 1978. 'The Ethiopian Revolution: A Hard Period', (An interview with B. Bayih), *World Marxist Review*, vol. XXI, no. 4, April.

Bequele, A. & Chole, E. 1969. *A Profile of the Ethiopian Economy*. Addis Ababa, Oxford University Press.

Bereket Habte Selassie 1980. *Conflict and Intervention in the Horn of Africa*. New York, Monthly Review.

Blechman, B. 1975. *The Control of Naval Armaments*. Washington, D.C., The Brookings Institution.

Brietzke, P. H. 1976, 'Land Reform in Revolutionary Ethiopia', *Journal of Modern African Studies*, vol. 14, no. 4.

— 1982. *Law, Development, and the Ethiopian Revolution*. Lewisburg, Bucknell University Press.

Cahill, K. M. 1979. 'Somalia: A Tragedy Beyond Cambodia's', *Horn of Africa*, vol. 2, no. 4.

Caputo, B. 1983. 'Ethiopia, Revolution in an Ancient Empire'. *National Geographic*, vol. 163, no. 5.

Castro, F. 1977. Interview, *Afrique-Asie*, 16 May.

Cohen, J. & Koehn, P. 1980. *Ethiopian Provincial and Municipal Government*. East Lansing, African Studies Center, Michigan State University.

— 1977. 'Rural and Urban Land Reform in Ethiopia', *African Law Studies*, vol. 14.

Constitución de la Republica de Cuba 1976. 25 February, Havana.

Edmonds, R. 1975. *Soviet Foreign Policy 1962-1973*. London, Oxford University Press.

Eritrean Liberation Front 1971. *Eritrea: A Victim of UN Decision and of Ethiopian Aggression*, 3 December, New York.

Eritrean People's Liberation Front 1977. *National Democratic Programme*, 31 January, Eritrea.

Ethiopia Profile 1982. vol. 1, no. 4.
— 1982. vol. 1, no. 2.
— 1982. vol. 1, nos. 7 & 8. (Gutema, 'Leadership Rivalry: Reality or Propaganda Ploy?').
Ethiopia Statistical Abstract 1966, 1970, 1971, 1972, 1973. Addis Ababa, Central Statistical Office.
Ethiopian Herald, 1976. 21 April.
— 1977. 5 February.
— 1980. 25 June.
— 1977. 18 November.
— 1977. 13 September.
Ethiopian National Democratic Revolution Programme 1976. 20 April, Addis Ababa.
Etzkowitz, H. & Schwab, P. 1976. *Is America Necessary?*. St. Paul, West.
Fanon, F. 1968. *The Wretched of the Earth*. New York, Grove.
Fitch, B. & Oppenheimer, M. 1966. *Ghana: End of an Illusion*. New York, Monthly Review.
Frank, A. G. 1981. *Crisis: In The Third World*. New York, Holmes & Meier.
GATT 1982. *International Trade 1981/2*. Geneva.
Gilkes, P. 1975. *The Dying Lion: Feudalism and Modernization in Ethiopia*. London, Julian Friedman.
Ginzberg, E. & Smith, H. 1967. *Manpower Strategy for Developing Countries: Lessons from Ethiopia*. New York, Columbia University Press.
Goddard, I. 1978. 'An Interview with Ethiopia's Foreign Minister', *Horn of Africa*, vol. 1, no. 2.
Gott, R. 1982. 'How Left and Right fiddled while Ethiopia burned'. *Guardian Weekly*, 14 February.
'Government Ownership of Urban Lands and Extra Houses Proclamation', 1975. 26 July, Addis Ababa, *Negarit Gazeta*.
Granma 1978. 22 January.
— 1981. 4 June.
— 1978. 7 May.
Greenfield, R. 1979. 'An historical introduction to refugee problems in the Horn'. *Horn of Africa*, vol. 2, no. 4.
Griswold, D. ed. 1978a. *The Ethiopian Revolution*. New York, World View.
— 1978b. *Eyewitness Ethiopia, The Continuing Revolution*. New York, World View.
Guevara, E. 1971. Notes for the study of the ideology of the Cuban revolution. In *Revolution: A Reader*, eds B. Mazlish, A. D. Kaledin & D. B. Ralston. New York, Macmillan.
Halliday, F. & Molyneux, M. 1981. *The Ethiopian Revolution*. London, Verso.
Hoben, A. 1973. *Land Tenure Among the Amhara of Ethiopia*. Chicago, The University of Chicago Press.
— 1975. 'Perspectives on land reform in Ethiopia: the political role of the peasantry'. *Rural Africana*, vol. 28.

International Monetary Fund 1982. *International Financial Statistics Yearbook.* December.
— 1983. *Monthly Bulletin of Statistics.* April.
Kapuscinski, R. 1983. *The Emperor: Downfall of an Autocrat.* New York, Harcourt Brace Jovanovich.
Labour Proclamation. 1975. Addis Ababa, *Negarit Gazeta.*
Legum, C. 1975. *Ethiopia: The Fall of Haile Selassie's Empire.* New York, Africana.
Legum, C. & Lee, B. 1977. *Conflict in the Horn of Africa.* New York, Africana.
Lenin, V. 1960. *State and Revolution.* Moscow, Foreign Languages Publishing House.
— 1968. *The Proletarian Revolution and the Renegade Kautsky.* In V. Lenin, *Selected Works,* vol.II, New York, International.
— 1970. *Questions of National Policy and Proletarian Internationalism.* Moscow, Progress.
— 1971. 'What is to be Done?' In Mazlish *et al.* (eds), *Revolution, A Reader.* New York, Macmillan.
Leslau, W. 1969. *Falasha Anthology.* New York, Schocken.
Levine, D. N. 1965. *Wax and Gold.* Chicago, The University of Chicago Press.
Lewis, I. M. 1977. 'Has the Dergue had its Day?' *The Guardian, London,* 21 August.
Mao Tse-tung 1962. *On Practice.* In *Mao Tse-tung: An Anthology of His Writings,* ed. A. Fremantle. New York, Mentor.
Marcuse, H. 1969. *An Essay on Liberation.* Boston, Beacon.
Markakis, J. & Ayele, N. 1978. *Class and Revolution in Ethiopia.* Nottingham, Spokesman.
Marx, K. & Engels, F. 1848. *The Communist Manifesto.*
Mazlish, B., Kaledin, A. D. & Ralston, D. B. 1971. *Revolution, A Reader.* New York, Macmillan.
Memmi, A. 1967. *The Colonizer and the Colonized.* Boston, Beacon.
Ministry of Foreign Affairs 1981. 'What Should Ethiopia's Guiding Foreign Policy Be at the Present Time?' *Horn of Africa,* vol. 4, no. 2.
NATO 1983. *Press Service,* 8 April, no. (83)6. Brussels.
Newsletter of Eritreans for Liberation in North America 1977. 'Eritrea in Struggle', vol. 1, no. 8.
New York Times 1983. 6 April.
— 1983. 22 April.
— 1983. 23 April.
— 1974. 21 December.
— 1977. 27 July.
— 1976. 13 September.
1982 Yearbook on International Communist Affairs. Stanford, Hoover Institution.
1983 Yearbook on International Communist Affairs. Stanford, Hoover Institution.
1984 Yearbook on International Communist Affairs. Stanford, Hoover Institution.
Ojo, O. 1980/81. 'Ethiopia's Foreign Policy Since the 1974 Revolution'. *Horn of Africa,* vol. 3, no. 4.
Ottaway, M. 1976. 'Social Classes and Corporate Interests in the Ethiopian Revolution'. *Journal of Modern African Studies,* vol. 14, no. 3.

Ottaway, M. 1982. *Soviet and American Influence in the Horn of Africa.* New York, Praeger.

Ottaway, M. & Ottaway, D. 1978. *Ethiopia, Empire in Revolution.* New York, Africana.

Oye, K. A. 1983. 'International Systems Structure and American Foreign Policy'. In K. A. Oye, R. J. Lieber & D. Rothchild (eds), *Eagle Defiant, United States Foreign Policy in the 1980s.* Boston, Little, Brown.

Policy Guidelines on Ethiopian Socialism 1974. 20 December, Addis Ababa.

Pollis, A. & Schwab, P. 1980. 'Human Rights, A Western Construct with Limited Applicability'. In A. Pollis & P. Schwab (eds), *Human Rights, Cultural and Ideological Perspectives.* New York, Praeger.

Pravda 1981. 19 June.

Proclamation of the Nationalization of Rural Land 1975. 4 March. Addis Ababa, *Negarit Gazeta.*

Rapoport, L. 1979. *The Lost Jews, Last of the Ethiopian Falashas.* New York, Stein and Day.

Reagan, R. 1983. *Central America,* Speech before a Joint-Session of the US Congress. 27 April, Washington, D.C.

Rothchild, D. & Ravenhill, J. 1983. 'From Carter to Reagan: The Global Perspective on Africa Becomes Ascendant'. In K. A. Oye, R. J. Leiber & D. Rothchild (eds), *Eagle Defiant, United States Foreign Policy in the 1980s.* Boston, Little, Brown.

Schlesinger, J. R. 1975. *Statement by the Secretary of Defence, Before the Senate Armed Services Committee.* 10 June. Senate, Washington, D.C.

School Census for Ethiopia. 1967, 1968, 1969, 1970, 1971, 1972, 1973. Addis Ababa, Ministry of Education and Fine Arts.

Schwab, P. 1978. 'Cold War on the Horn of Africa'. *African Affairs,* vol. 77, no. 306.

— 1972. *Decision-Making in Ethiopia.* London, C. Hurst.

— 1979. *Haile Selassie I: Ethiopia's Lion of Judah.* Chicago, Nelson-Hall.

— 1981. 'Socialist Ethiopia'. In *Marxist Governments, A World Survey,* vol. 2, ed. B. Szajkowski. London, Macmillan.

— 1982. 'The Response of the Left to Violence and Human Rights "Abuses" in the Ethiopian Revolution'. In P. Schwab & A. Pollis (eds), *Toward a Human Rights Framework.* New York, Praeger.

Shepherd, J. 1975. *The Politics of Starvation.* Washington, D.C., Carnegie Endowment for International Peace.

Sherman, R. 1980. *Eritrea, The Unfinished Revolution.* New York, Praeger.

Singer, N. J. 1978. 'Legal Development in Post-Revolutionary Ethiopia'. *Horn of Africa,* vol. 1, no. 2.

Stalin, J. 1948. *Sochinenya,* V. 8, Moscow.

Stevens, R. P. 1976. 'The 1972 Addis Ababa Agreement and the Sudan's Afro-Arab Policy'. *Journal of Modern African Studies,* vol. 14, no. 2.

Swiss Review of World Affairs 1981. May, Geneva.

Syncrisis: The Dynamics of Health, Ethiopia 1974. Vol. VIII, Washington, D.C., US Department of Health, Education and Welfare.

Szajkowski, B. (ed.), 1981. *Marxist Governments, A World Survey,* vol. 2. London, Macmillan.

Ten-Year Investment Programme 1981. Addis Ababa.

'Tragedy in the Horn' 1981. *Horn of Africa*, vol. 4, no. 1, pp. 5-84.

Turner, S. 1977. 'The Naval Balance: Not Just a Numbers Game'. *Foreign Affairs*, vol. 55, no. 2.

United Nations 1982. *Report of the U.N. High Commission for Refugees.* General Assembly Supplement, Official Records, 37th Session, # 12(A/37/12). New York.

United Nations Food and Agriculture Organization 1974. *A Policy and Plan for Improving Food Security in Ethiopia*, July, Rome.

US Security Agreements and Commitments Abroad, Ethiopia 1970. Committee on Foreign Relations, US Senate. Part 8, June 1.

Uwechue, R. 1978. Interview with Mengistu Haile Mariam. In *Africa*, vol. LXXIX.

Vivo, R. V. 1978. *Ethiopia's Revolution.* New York, International.

Weiss, S. 1974. *Statement Before the House Foreign Affairs Sub-Committee on the Middle East and South Asia.* US Congress, April 10.

World Bank 1980. *World Development Report.*

— 1981. *World Development Report.*

— 1983. *World Development Report.*

Yusuf, A. A. 1980. 'The Anglo-Abyssinian Treaty of 1897 and the Somali-Ethiopian Dispute'. *Horn of Africa*, vol. 3, no. 1.

Index